Building Real-Time Analytics Systems

From Events to Insights with
Apache Kafka and Apache Pinot

Mark Needham
Foreword by Gunnar Morling

Beijing · Boston · Farnham · Sebastopol · Tokyo

Building Real-Time Analytics Systems

by Mark Needham

Copyright © 2023 Blue Theta and Dunith Dhanushka. All rights reserved.

Published by O'Reilly Media, Inc., 1005 Gravenstein Highway North, Sebastopol, CA 95472.

O'Reilly books may be purchased for educational, business, or sales promotional use. Online editions are also available for most titles (*https://oreilly.com*). For more information, contact our corporate/institutional sales department: 800-998-9938 or *corporate@oreilly.com*.

Acquisitions Editor: Michelle Smith
Development Editor: Shira Evans
Production Editor: Jonathon Owen
Copyeditor: Penelope Perkins
Proofreader: Sharon Wilkey

Indexer: nSight, Inc.
Interior Designer: David Futato
Cover Designer: Karen Montgomery
Illustrator: Kate Dullea

September 2023:   First Edition

Revision History for the First Edition
2023-09-13:   First Release

See *https://oreilly.com/catalog/errata.csp?isbn=9781098138790* for release details.

978-1-098-13879-0

[LSI]

Table of Contents

Foreword

When I started my career in software engineering in the early 2000s, data analytics oftentimes was an afterthought when designing software systems. Batch jobs running once per day would extract data from operational databases and load it into data warehouses, and business analysts typically were happy when they could look at the data from yesterday or last week, creating reports, running once-off queries, etc.

Apart from perhaps a few handcrafted, highly optimized queries running within operational databases, the idea of user-facing analytics was pretty much unheard of: serving analytics workloads to thousands of concurrent users, based on the freshest data possible. Since then, the appetite for real-time analytics has substantially increased. Use cases like fraud detection, resource planning, content recommendations, predictive analytics, and many others require the latest data in order to provide value. If, for instance, your bank detects a pattern of misuse for your credit card because it got stolen, you'd want your card to be blocked right now and not tomorrow, right?

Tools and platforms such as Apache Kafka (for data streaming), Apache Flink (stream processing), Apache Pinot (data analytics) and Apache Superset (data visualization) provide an excellent foundation for real-time analytics and have seen a tremendous uptake over the last years. At the same time, getting started with implementing your first use cases can be challenging, and you might ask yourself questions such as these: Which tools to choose for which purpose? How to put the individual pieces together for a coherent solution? What challenges exist when putting them into production and how to overcome those?

Mark's book is a treasure trove of guidance around these and many other concerns. Starting with the foundations (What even is real-time analytics?), he provides a comprehensive overview of the software ecosystem in this space, discusses Apache Pinot as one of the leading real-time analytics platforms, and dives into production considerations as well as more specific aspects such geospatial queries and upsert operations (a notoriously tricky part in most analytics stores).

Having worked on Debezium, an open source platform for change data capture (CDC), for many years, it's my particular joy to see an entire chapter on that topic. CDC plays a key role in real-time data pipelines, with feeding live data changes from operational databases such as MySQL or PostgreSQL to analytics platforms like Apache Pinot being a core use case, which I've seen coming up again and again in the Debezium community. Being an experienced CDC user himself, Mark is doing an excellent job explaining key CDC use cases and implementation approaches and showing how to set up Debezium in a comprehensive example.

The great attention to detail and practical hands-on style are a defining theme of the entire book: any conceptual discussion is always followed by practical examples, showing the reader in detail how to put the different ideas and technologies into action. The book is great for reading end to end, or you can equally well just pick specific chapters if you want to learn more about one particular topic.

The world around us is real-time, and any software systems we build need to account for that fact. As you implement your own analytics use cases for gaining real-time insight into your data, *Building Real-Time Analytics Systems* will quickly become an invaluable resource, and I am sure it's going to keep its spot on your desk for quick access for a long time.

— Gunnar Morling
Hamburg, June 2023

Preface

This book is a practical guide for implementing real-time analytics applications on top of existing data infrastructure. It is aimed at data engineers, data architects, and application developers who have some experience working with streaming data or would like to get acquainted with it.

In Chapters 1 and 2, we give an introduction to the topic and an overview of the types of real-time analytics applications that you can build. We also describe the types of products/tools that you'll likely be using, explaining how to pick the right tool for the job, as well as explaining when a tool might not be necessary.

In Chapter 3, we introduce a fictional pizza company that already has streaming infrastructure set up but hasn't yet implemented any real-time functionality. The next seven chapters will show how to implement different types of real-time analytics applications for this pizza company. If you're interested in getting your hands dirty, these chapters will be perfect for you, and hopefully you'll pick up some ideas (and code!) that you can use in your own projects.

The book will conclude with considerations when putting applications into production, a look at some real-world use cases of real-time analytics, and a gaze into our real-time analytics crystal ball to see what might be coming in this field over the next few years.

Conventions Used in This Book

The following typographical conventions are used in this book:

Italic
> Indicates new terms, URLs, email addresses, filenames, and file extensions.

Constant width

> Used for program listings, as well as within paragraphs to refer to program elements such as variable or function names, databases, data types, environment variables, statements, and keywords.

Constant width bold

> Shows commands or other text that should be typed literally by the user.

Constant width italic

> Shows text that should be replaced with user-supplied values or by values determined by context.

 This element signifies a tip or suggestion.

 This element signifies a general note.

Using Code Examples

Supplemental material (code examples, exercises, etc.) is available for download at *https://oreil.ly/RTA-github*.

If you have a technical question or a problem using the code examples, please send email to *bookquestions@oreilly.com*.

This book is here to help you get your job done. In general, if example code is offered with this book, you may use it in your programs and documentation. You do not need to contact us for permission unless you're reproducing a significant portion of the code. For example, writing a program that uses several chunks of code from this book does not require permission. Selling or distributing examples from O'Reilly books does require permission. Answering a question by citing this book and quoting example code does not require permission. Incorporating a significant amount of example code from this book into your product's documentation does require permission.

We appreciate, but generally do not require, attribution. An attribution usually includes the title, author, publisher, and ISBN. For example: "*Building Real-Time Analytics Systems* by Mark Needham (O'Reilly). Copyright 2023 Blue Theta and Dunith Dhanushka, 978-1-098-13879-0."

If you feel your use of code examples falls outside fair use or the permission given above, feel free to contact us at *permissions@oreilly.com*.

O'Reilly Online Learning

O'REILLY® For more than 40 years, *O'Reilly Media* has provided technology and business training, knowledge, and insight to help companies succeed.

Our unique network of experts and innovators share their knowledge and expertise through books, articles, and our online learning platform. O'Reilly's online learning platform gives you on-demand access to live training courses, in-depth learning paths, interactive coding environments, and a vast collection of text and video from O'Reilly and 200+ other publishers. For more information, visit *https://oreilly.com*.

How to Contact Us

Please address comments and questions concerning this book to the publisher:

O'Reilly Media, Inc.
1005 Gravenstein Highway North
Sebastopol, CA 95472
800-889-8969 (in the United States or Canada)
707-829-7019 (international or local)
707-829-0104 (fax)
support@oreilly.com
https://www.oreilly.com/about/contact.html

We have a web page for this book, where we list errata, examples, and any additional information. You can access this page at *https://oreil.ly/building-RTA*.

For news and information about our books and courses, visit *https://oreilly.com*.

Find us on LinkedIn: *https://linkedin.com/company/oreilly-media*

Follow us on Twitter: *https://twitter.com/oreillymedia*

Watch us on YouTube: *https://youtube.com/oreillymedia*

Acknowledgments

Writing this book has been an exhilarating journey, and I am deeply grateful to the countless individuals who have provided their support, wisdom, and encouragement along the way.

First and foremost, I would like to extend my heartfelt appreciation to Dunith Dhanushka, a prominent thought leader in the real-time analytics space. His insightful blog posts and engaging talk at Current 2022 have served as invaluable sources of inspiration, shaping significant portions of this book. The opportunity to engage in thought-provoking conversations with him has not only deepened my understanding of the intricacies of the real-time analytics stack but also guided me in refining the way I presented these concepts throughout the manuscript.

I am also immensely grateful to Hubert Dulay, who generously shared his expertise as a technical reviewer for this book. His keen eyes and astute suggestions have been crucial in ensuring the accuracy and clarity of the content presented. Hubert's dedication to providing constructive feedback has played a vital role in enhancing the overall quality of the book, and I am truly thankful for his invaluable contributions.

CHAPTER 1

Introduction to Real-Time Analytics

> It's a huge competitive advantage to see in real time what's happening with your data.
>
> —Hilary Mason, Founder and CEO of Fast Forward Labs

A lot of data in a business environment is considered unbounded because it arrives gradually over time. Customers, employers, and machines produced data yesterday and today and will continue to produce more data tomorrow. This process never ends unless you go out of business, so the dataset is never complete in any meaningful way.

 Of the companies that participated in Confluent's Business Impact of Data Streaming: State of Data in Motion Report 2022 (*https://oreil.ly/pGIMb*), 97% have access to real-time data streams, and 66% have widespread access.

Today, many businesses are adopting streaming data and real-time analytics to make faster, more reliable, and more accurate decisions, allowing them to gain a competitive advantage in their market segment.

This chapter provides an introduction to streaming and real-time analytics. We'll start with a refresher about streaming data before explaining why organizations want to apply analytics on top of that data. After going through some use cases, we'll conclude with an overview of the types of real-time analytics applications we can build.

What Is an Event Stream?

The term *streaming* describes a continuous, never-ending flow of data. The data is made available incrementally over time, which means that you can act upon it without needing to wait for the whole dataset to become available so that you can download it.

A *data stream* consists of a series of data points ordered in time, that is, chronological order, as shown in Figure 1-1.

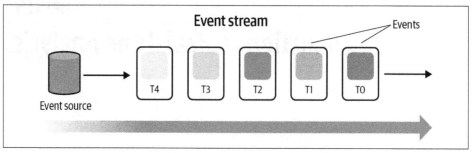

Figure 1-1. A data stream

Each data point represents an *event*, or a change in the state of the business. For example, these might be real-time events like a stream of transactions coming from an organization or Internet of Things (IoT) sensors emitting their readings.

One thing even streams have in common is that they keep on producing data for as long as the business exists. Event streams are generated by different data sources in a business, in various formats and volumes.

We can also consider a data stream as an immutable, time-ordered stream of events, carrying facts about state changes that occurred in the business. These sources include, but are not limited to, ecommerce purchases, in-game player activity, information from social networks, clickstream data, activity logs from web servers, sensor data, and telemetry from connected devices or instrumentation in data centers.

An example of an event is the following:

A user with ID 1234 purchased item 567 for $3.99 on 2022/06/12 at 12:23:212

Events are an immutable representation of facts that happened in the past. The facts of this event are shown in Table 1-1.

Table 1-1. Facts in event example

Fact	Value
User ID	1234
Item purchased	567
Price paid	$3.99

By aggregating and analyzing event streams, businesses can uncover insights about their customers and use them to improve their offerings. In the next section, we will discuss different means of making sense of events.

Making Sense of Streaming Data

Events have a shelf life. The business value of events rapidly decreases over time, as shown in Figure 1-2.

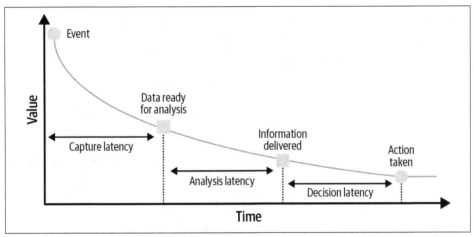

Figure 1-2. Event shelf life

The sooner you understand events' behavior, the sooner you can react and maximize your business outcome. For example, if we have an event that a user abandoned their shopping cart, we can reach out to them via SMS or email to find out why that happened. Perhaps we can offer them a voucher for one of the items in their cart to entice them to come back and complete the transaction.

But that only works if we're able to react to the cart abandonment in real time. If we detect it tomorrow, the user has probably forgotten what they were doing and will likely ignore our email.

What Is Real-Time Analytics?

Real-time analytics (RTA) describes an approach to data processing that allows us to extract value from events as soon as they are made available.

> When we use the term *real time* in this book, we are referring to soft real time. Delays causes by network latencies and garbage collection pauses, for example, may delay the delivery and processing of events by hundreds of milliseconds or more.

Real-time analytics differs substantially from *batch processing*, where we collect data in batches and then process it, often with quite a long delay between event time and processing time. Figure 1-3 gives a visual representation of batch processing.

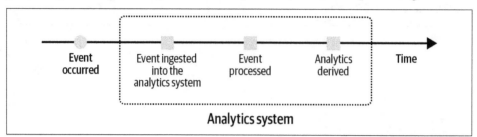

Figure 1-3. Batch processing

In contrast, with real-time analytics we react right after the event happens, as shown in Figure 1-4.

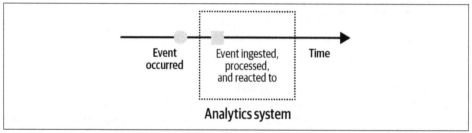

Figure 1-4. Real-time processing

Traditionally, batch processing was the only means of data analysis, but it required us to draw artificial time boundaries to make it easier to divide the data into chunks of fixed duration and process them in batches. For example, we might process a day's worth of data at the end of every day or an hour's worth of data at the end of every hour. That was too slow for many users because it produced stale results and didn't allow them to react to things as they were happening.

Over time the impact of these problems was reduced by decreasing the size of processing batches down to the minute or even the second, which eventually led to events being processed as they arrived and fixed time slices being abandoned. And that is the whole idea behind real-time analytics!

Real-time analytics systems capture, analyze, and act upon events as soon as they become available. They are the unbounded, incrementally processed counterpart to the batch processing systems that have dominated the data analytics space for years.

Benefits of Real-Time Analytics

Speed is a decisive factor in decision making, where organizations that are fast enough to understand and respond to events more often become market leaders, while others remain followers. Therefore, a real-time analytics system can be beneficial to business in many ways, as shown in Figure 1-5.

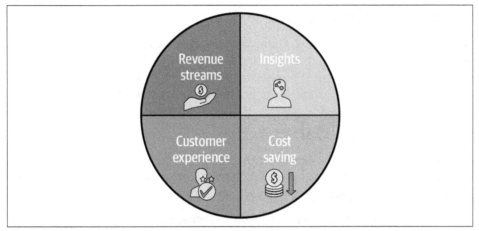

Figure 1-5. Benefits of real-time analytics

In this section, we will explore several benefits of real-time analytics systems.

New Revenue Streams

Real-time analytics can generate new revenue streams for organizations in a couple of different ways. By allowing end users to have access to analytical querying capabilities, organizations can develop brand new data-centered products that are compelling enough that users will pay to have access.

In addition, real-time analytics can make existing applications more compelling, leading to increased user engagement and retention, as well as driving more usage of the application, ultimately creating more revenue for the organization.

Timely Access to Insights

Real-time analytics enables better, faster, and improved decision making by providing timely access to actionable insights. Businesses can maximize their profits and reduce losses by understanding and reacting to events in real time. For example, real-time customer behavior analysis results in launching dynamic and more focused marketing campaigns, which often drive high returns. Also, a real-time temperature-monitoring system can reduce costs by shutting down air conditioning based on fluctuations in temperature.

Reduced Infrastructure Cost

In traditional batch processing, data storage and computation is often coupled, resulting in an exponential growth in infrastructure cost as the data volume grows over time. In real-time analytics, data is processed as it arrives, eliminating the need for costly data storage and processing systems.

Improved Overall Customer Experience

Addressing customer issues took a rather reactive approach in the past, as issues were reported, diagnosed, and solved in lengthy time frames. With real-time analytics, businesses can proactively attend to customers by constantly monitoring for potential issues and fixing them automatically, improving overall customer satisfaction.

Real-Time Analytics Use Cases

Real-time analytics is not a new thing. It has been around in many industries for quite some time. In this section, we will look at several real-world use cases where real-time analytics is applicable and has already been delivering value to businesses.

There are a variety of use cases for real-time analytics, and each use case has different requirements with respect to query throughput, query latency, query complexity, and data accuracy. A real-time metrics use case requires higher data accuracy, but it's fine if queries take a bit longer to return. On the other hand, a user-facing analytical application must be optimized for query speed.

Table 1-2 describes some use cases and their query properties.

Table 1-2. Common use cases and their properties

Use case	Query throughput (queries/second)	Query latency (p95th)	Consistency & accuracy	Query complexity
User-facing analytics	Very high	Very low	Best effort	Low
Personalization	Very high	Very low	Best effort	Low
Metrics	High	Very low	Accurate	Low
Anomaly detection	Moderate	Very low	Best effort	Low
Root-cause analytics	High	Very low	Best effort	Low
Visualizations & dashboarding	Moderate	Low	Best effort	Medium
Ad hoc analytics	Low	High	Best effort	High
Log analytics & text search	Moderate	Moderate	Best effort	Medium

User-Facing Analytics

Organizations have been generating and collecting massive amounts of data for a long time now. Analytics on that data has been playing a crucial role in analyzing user behavior, growth potential, and revenue spend, enabling employees and executives to make key business decisions.

This analytics has mostly been done inside organizations, but there is an increasing desire to provide this analytical capability directly to end users. Doing so will democratize decision making and provide an even more personalized experience. The term *user-facing analytics* has been coined to describe this process.

The key requirements are high throughput and low query latency, since this directly impacts the user experience.

Personalization

Personalization is a special type of user-facing analytics used to personalize the product experience for a given user. This might mean showing them content that they'll be particularly interested in or presenting them with vouchers specific to their interests.

This is done by going through a user's activity and product interaction and extracting real-time features, which are then used to generate personalized recommendations or actions.

Metrics

Tracking business metrics in real time allows us to get an up-to-date view on key performance indicators (KPIs). This enables organizations to identify issues and take proactive steps to address them in a timely manner.

Being able to do this is particularly critical for operational intelligence, anomaly/fraud detection, and financial planning.

This use case has a requirement for a high number of queries per second along with low latency. We must also achieve a high degree of data accuracy.

Anomaly Detection and Root Cause Analysis

Anomaly detection and root cause analysis is a popular use case when working with time-series data. *Time-series data* is a sequence of data points collected over a period of time.

In the context of ecommerce, this could include data like the number of transactions per day, average transaction value, or number of returns.

Anomaly detection is all about identifying unusual patterns in data that may indicate a problem that we need to address. That problem might be a sudden surge in orders of a particular product or even that fraudulent activity is being committed.

Either way, we need to find out what went wrong quickly. It's no use finding out that we had a problem 24 hours ago—we need to know about it now!

And once we've detected that something unusual has happened, we also need to understand which dimensions were responsible for any anomalies. In other words, we need to find the root cause of the issue.

This use case performs temporal scans and *Group By* queries at a high number of queries per second.

Visualization

Much has been said about the death of the dashboard (*https://oreil.ly/2wL5o*), but dashboards still have a role to play in the real-time analytics space.

This could be as simple as a dashboard that plots metrics on different charts or as complex as geospatial visualization, clustering, trend analysis, and more. The main difference from a typical dashboard is that tables and charts will be constantly updated as new data comes in.

The serving layer must integrate with existing visualization solutions like Apache Superset and Grafana.

Ad Hoc Analytics

Analysts often want to do real-time data exploration to debug issues and detect patterns as events are being ingested. This means that we need to be able to run SQL queries against the serving layer.

Analysts will also want to do some analysis that combines real-time data with historical data. For example, they might want to see how the business is performing this month compared to the same month in previous years. This means that we either need to bring the historical data into the serving layer or use a distributed SQL query engine that can combine multiple data sources. The number of queries per second will be slow, but query complexity is likely to be high.

Log Analytics/Text Search

Running real-time text search queries on application log data is a less common but still important use case. Since logs are often unstructured, we must be able to run regex-style text search on this data to triage production issues.

The queries per second will be low for most applications, but will get higher if we are debugging a user-facing application.

Classifying Real-Time Analytics Applications

Now that you've been introduced to streaming data and real-time analytics, along with its benefits and several industry use cases, the remaining chapters of the book will walk through the process of building real-time analytics applications to harness value from streaming data.

Before starting to build, let's classify real-time analytics applications based on the audience and the use cases they serve. That helps us pick the right application type to solve our analytics needs.

The quadrant diagram shown in Figure 1-6 divides real-time analytics applications into four categories along two axes.

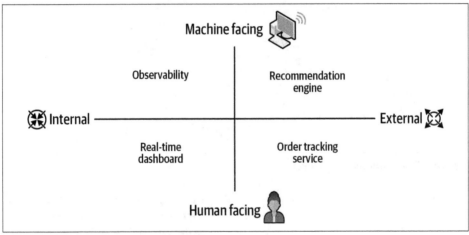

Figure 1-6. Real-time analytics quadrants

Internal Versus External Facing

There are two types of real-time analytics applications: internal and external facing.

Internal facing means the insights produced by applications are utilized within organizational boundaries, possibly for internal use cases. An example would be a transportation company monitoring vehicle performance to optimize fuel efficiency and detect maintenance issues, or a telecommunications provider that monitors network performance and network capacity.

External facing means that the insights are consumed by an audience external to the organization, possibly by end users. Examples would be a user of a ride-sharing application tracking the ride's location in real time or a health-care app that tracks patient vital signs in real time and alerts health-care professionals to any changes that require attention.

Traditionally, many more applications have been built for internal users because doing so is easier. The number of users concurrently accessing an internal application is usually relatively small, and they also have a higher tolerance for query latency—if a query takes 10 seconds to run, so be it.

External users, on the other hand, aren't nearly as forgiving. They expect queries to return results instantly, and there are many more of these users accessing a given application, all of whom will likely be using the system at the same time. On the other hand, serving real-time analytics to external users gives us a big opportunity, as shown in Figure 1-7.

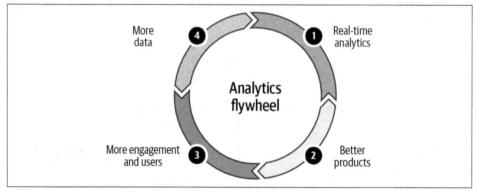

Figure 1-7. The analytics flywheel

Real-time analytics improves the products that we're offering to external users. This in turn means that more of them will use and engage with those products, in the process generating more data, which we can use to create new products.

Machine Versus Human Facing

The analytics produced by *human-facing* applications are delivered using a UI, such as a dashboard, and consumed by humans, including decision-makers, analysts, operators, engineers, and end users. Ad hoc interactive exploration of insights is the primary objective of these applications.

Machine-facing analytics applications are consumed by machines, such as microservices, recommendation engines, and machine learning algorithms. There, the logic to derive analytics is programmed into the application prior to the execution, eliminating any human intervention. Speed and accuracy are primary objectives of machine-facing applications, where humans often fail to deliver at scale.

Summary

In this chapter, we learned how streams of events form the foundation for real-time analytics, a practice of analyzing events as soon as they are made available. We also discussed the benefits of real-time analytics, along with a few industry use cases. Finally, we classified real-time analytics applications based on the audience they are serving.

In the next chapter, we will dive deep into the real-time analytics landscape to identify critical components that exist in a typical real-time analytics infrastructure.

CHAPTER 2

The Real-Time Analytics Ecosystem

In the previous chapter, we discussed the fundamentals of real-time analytics: the events, streams, and different types of real-time analytics systems. Real-time analytics is a vast domain consisting of multiple tools, technologies, and practices. Before building real-time analytics applications, it will be crucial for you to identify the technology ecosystem around real-time analytics. The related tools and technologies work together to derive insights from streaming data.

In this chapter, we go back in time and discuss the first-generation real-time analytics systems, their early days, the influence of the Lambda architecture, and the challenges they faced. Then we discuss the modern real-time analytics ecosystem (or the modern streaming stack), its composition, and its outlook for the future.

We hope that by the end of this chapter, you will have a map that you can use to analyze any future data infrastructure products and understand where they fit into the real-time analytics application architecture.

Defining the Real-Time Analytics Ecosystem

Imagine you are building an ecommerce web application and have to play multiple roles as architect, backend developer, and operator. As an architect, you will decide on factors like cloud provider and geographical region, container orchestration mechanism, and high-availability requirements. As a backend developer, you will not only write the application code but also work closely with other overlapping components that impact the application. For example, you will configure the database, define schemas, configure the identity provider, and design, create, and publish APIs. As an operator, you will instrument the application for monitoring and set up the continuous integration/continuous delivery (CI/CD) pipeline.

For each role you play, you will work with a specific set of tools and technologies. That is what we call your application's *technology ecosystem*—a set of related tools and technologies working closely to deliver a business use case (see Figure 2-1).

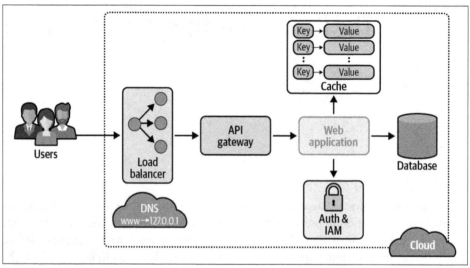

Figure 2-1. Ecosystem of a typical web application

The same applies to real-time analytics applications. Whether you are a beginner or an experienced practitioner, it is important to understand the technology ecosystem of real-time analytics applications. Essentially, that requires you to be aware of the data flow of the application and the technologies that intercept that data flow while the application is in operation. Simply put, it means identifying the components where the data flow originates, the components that move and process data, and, finally, the destinations where the insights are derived from moving data.

We can define that as the *real-time analytics ecosystem*--the tools, processes, and technologies used to derive insights from unbounded streams of data. The terms *real-time analytics stack* and *streaming stack* mean the same thing and are used interchangeably in the industry.

Whether you are an architect, developer, or operator, knowing the streaming stack helps you design, build, and operate robust and performant real-time analytics applications. We will explore the streaming stack in detail in the following sections.

The Classic Streaming Stack

It's common for technology ecosystems to evolve over time so that they find better versions of themselves. For example, the automobiles we see today are very different from the cars of the early 20th century. The same goes for the real-time analytics ecosystem: the streaming stack we see today is quite different from its early days. In this section, we will explore the classic streaming stack—the technology ecosystem we used to have a couple of decades ago—and why it failed to capture a wider portion of the market.

The origin of real-time analytics dates back to the 1990s, where we had real-time analytics in the form of complex event processing (CEP) (*https://oreil.ly/X3L7J*).

Complex Event Processing

CEP started off as a bunch of academic research projects at Stanford University, the California Institute of Technology, and Cambridge University. Commercial products then derived from this work.

Conceptually, CEP is the opposite of querying a database to detect a pattern in the data. With CEP, you first define a pattern in the CEP engine and then send a stream of events in real time. As the events pass through, the CEP engine matches them against the registered pattern and then emits the matched events as a stream of complex events, hence the name *complex event processing*. A diagram of a CEP system is shown in Figure 2-2.

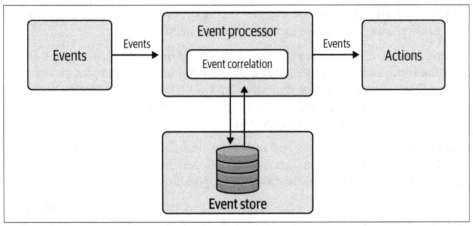

Figure 2-2. Complex event processing architecture

CEP (*https://oreil.ly/HJogN*) was widely used in several industry use cases, including fraud detection in financial services, monitoring anomalies in sensor networks, as well as general business activity monitoring. Vendors like Progress Apama, IBM InfoSphere Streams, TIBCO StreamBase, and WSO2 Siddhi all tried to bring CEP into the mass market, but with limited success. Unfortunately, CEP didn't have a standard approach, and its inherent complexity meant that it never achieved widespread adoption.

The Big Data Era

Next, we have the big data era, which began in the early 2010s. By this point, there had been exponential growth in data volume, velocity, and variety caused by new developments like the Internet of Things and innovations in machine learning and artificial intelligence that resulted in applications producing massive amounts of semi-structured and unstructured data. Conventional CEP systems were not built to deal with this volume of data and, unsurprisingly, were unable to handle it.

As a result, engineers started to develop a new class of real-time analytic systems.

This led to technologies like Kafka, which was originally built at LinkedIn as a high-throughput distributed message bus. It could ingest millions of events per second and store them across multiple nodes for fault tolerance. Kafka was later donated to the Apache Software Foundation, making it accessible to a wider developer community to build event-streaming applications.

Apache Samza and Apache Storm were two other prominent projects developed at this time. Apache Samza, also initially developed by LinkedIn, was designed to handle large amounts of data in real time and provide fault-tolerant, durable stateful computations. Apache Storm was created by Nathan Marz as part of the analytics platform at BackType, a startup that focused on real-time analytics and insights for social media data. BackType was eventually acquired by Twitter in 2011.

Around this time, Twitter was gaining prominence as the world's town square, and in 2012 the company rolled out a feature called *real-time trending topics*, powered by Apache Storm. Trending topics showed an up-to-the-minute view of what people on the platform were talking about in an attempt to create more interaction on the website. You can see a screenshot in Figure 2-3.

Twitter's top trends feature was responsible for introducing the concept of real-time analytics to many organizations. Marz also developed the lambda architecture, which became the basis of all the real-time analytics applications built around this time.

The lambda architecture is a popular architectural pattern for building large-scale data processing systems that could handle real-time data streams as well as batch data processing. It acted as a solution to the limitations of traditional batch processing systems and real-time processing systems.

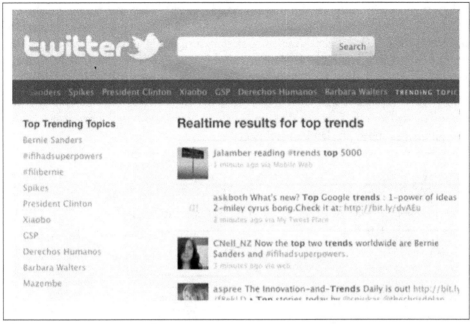

Figure 2-3. Twitter top trends

The lambda architecture is comprised of three layers:

Batch layer
A batch processing system like Apache Hadoop. It's responsible for processing large volumes of data in parallel in batch mode.

Speed layer
A stream processor like Storm. It's responsible for processing real-time data streams.

Serving layer
A read-optimized database, such as Apache HBase, that stores the output produced from other layers. It provides a unified view of both the batch and real-time data streams.

When events arrive, they are fed into the batch and speed layers simultaneously. The batch layer runs periodic ETL (extract, transform, load) jobs and creates preaggregated batch views. The speed layer runs stream processing jobs on recent data that hasn't been seen by the batch layer. The output of both layers is then written to the serving layer, which now has consolidated output from the other layers.

Things get complicated when a query comes into the serving layer, which has to stitch together data from the batch and real-time views before serving the results to the client. Figure 2-4 shows the lambda architecture.

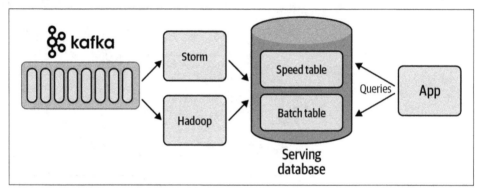

Figure 2-4. Lambda architecture

The main benefit of the lambda architecture is that it keeps the original input dataset intact, allowing it to be reprocessed later with a different processing logic. This means you can test and debug the application code at speed and batch layers repeatedly, allowing the code to evolve.

The lambda architecture saw reasonable adoption by Fortune 500 and internet-scale companies, but it didn't really get picked up by small and medium-sized organizations or early-stage startups, which also had a craving for real-time analytics. Why?

We believe that this architecture had limited adoption for three main reasons:

Overly complicated technology
> Technologies like Storm require you to master specialized skills such as distributed systems principles and performance engineering. Using Storm meant that you needed the capacity to operate what were effectively three distributed systems, one for each of the layers. This required not only more engineers to operate the distributed systems, but also the resources to provision more hardware and software as well.

JVM dependency
> Almost all notable stream processors were built on top of JVM languages like Java and Scala, requiring you to learn JVM specifics like JVM performance

tuning and debugging of memory issues. This ruled out adoption for many companies whose developers were used to coding in Python, C#, or Ruby.

Duplicated processing logic

You must build, test, and maintain the code at both the batch and speed layers, which are complicated distributed systems. The code must deliver the same result at the end, but the effort is duplicated.

All of this leads us to the modern streaming stack that we have today.

The Modern Streaming Stack

In this section, we will look at the real-time analytics application ecosystem at a very high level to identify the critical components and their responsibilities. As well as exploring each component in its own right, we'll also look at the ways that components interact with each other.

Real-time insights aren't achieved as the result of one component but rather as a coordinated effort between different components. You should therefore have a high-level idea of the real-time analytics ecosystem, covering at a minimum the components responsible for data production, storage, insights generation, and insights consumption. Ideally, you should have them sketched out on a whiteboard before even writing a single line of code.

You might be wondering why we put the word "modern" in front of "streaming stack." Figure 2-5 shows several reasons for this.

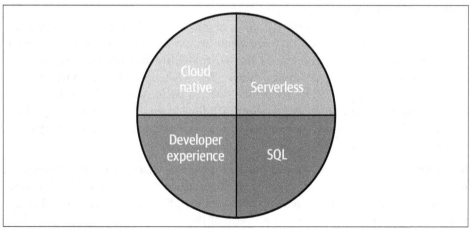

Figure 2-5. The modern streaming stack

The modern streaming stack has the following components:

Cloud native tools

The stack has been designed for modern cloud native tools; the components in the stack are designed to utilize the infinite compute and storage facilities available from modern cloud platforms. They are also designed to be deployed on Kubernetes and container environments to get the most out of scalability and availability requirements.

Managed and serverless platforms

Most of the stack components have self-serve managed options on popular cloud platforms. That's a massive advantage compared to the early days of the modern classic stack, where you had to deploy everything—Hadoop clusters, Hadoop Distributed File System (HDFS), and on-premises data centers. Managed self-serve platforms take away the management overhead, and things like observability are built in. No longer do you have to do your own logging, tracing, or measuring of latency between event hops—the platform takes care of all of that.

Rich tooling and developer experience

Modern components are also great for developers, who have rich tooling and a smooth developer experience available. Most of these tools natively support local testing and debugging, built-in observability, and seamless integration with CI tools for faster deployment cycles. Many of these tools will let you deploy with a single command. These benefits were rare in the early real-time analytics systems.

Expressive programming model

Finally, we have an expressive programming model. With tools in the classic streaming stack, any code that you wrote would be in an imperative programming language like Java or Scala. Those languages are imperative in the sense that you focus on how to do things rather than what needs to be done. Many of today's tools support SQL as a primary access point. Using SQL means we can focus on what needs to be done rather than how to do it, but an even bigger benefit is that it opens the door to many more developers, as almost everyone is familiar with SQL.

In summary, the modern streaming stack is the classic streaming stack reimagined with self-service cloud native tools, providing a simplified yet powerful developer experience to build real-time analytics applications. The new stack is inspired by the Kappa architecture, proposed by Jay Kreps in 2014.

Everything is modeled around events, and unlike the lambda architecture, we don't have two processing layers. Figure 2-6 gives an overview of the components that we'll explore in this chapter. You won't necessarily need to use all these components for every application, but you'll certainly be using some of them some of the time.

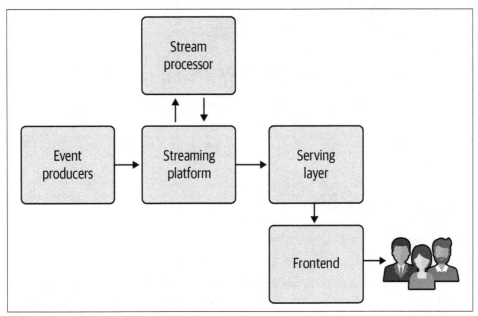

Figure 2-6. Real-time analytics stack

For each of the components, we'll explain the crucial characteristics to take into account when selecting a tool for that role, and we'll give a brief overview of some of the most popular implementations.

Event Producers

Event producers detect state changes in source systems and trigger events that can be consumed and processed by downstream applications. For example, in an ecommerce system, an order management system may trigger an `OrderReceived` event once it receives an order from the ecommerce frontend. This event may contain information such as order details, customer information, or transaction details.

There are three classes of event producers, as shown in Figure 2-7.

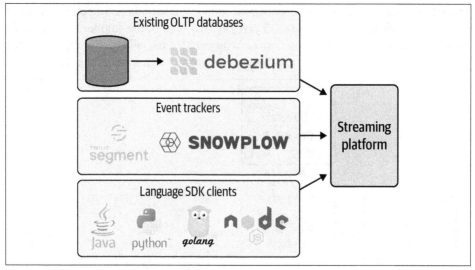

Figure 2-7. Event producers

Let's go through each type of event producer:

Existing OLTP databases
When it comes to operational data stuck in transactional databases, we can use *change data capture (CDC)* to stream that data into a streaming data platform for further analysis. CDC allows real-time replication of data changes from a source database to a target system, without affecting the source database's performance. In this area, Debezium has become the de facto standard in capturing row-level changes and streaming them to an event streaming platform in real time. It supports several popular databases, including MySQL, PostgreSQL, and MongoDB.

Event trackers
Event trackers let you capture events based on user interactions in web and mobile applications. They give you a platform and an SDK that you can use to instrument/annotate your event producer code. All you have to do is raise the event, and then they'll take care of capturing the event and transporting it to the streaming data platform. Exception handling, packaging the messages, and back-pressure are all handled. Two of the most popular event trackers are Segment and Snowplow.

Language SDK clients

If you want more control over the event production process, you might instead choose to use a language-specific SDK. The benefit of using a language SDK client is that you'll be able to define the serialization format, control batching, and control queue limits. The streaming data platforms offer language-specific SDKs for the major programming languages. For example, Apache Kafka has SDKs for Java, Python, Go, C#, and more.

Streaming Data Platform

The *streaming data platform* is the most critical component in the stack. This system acts as the source of truth for event data, and it must therefore be able to handle high volume and concurrency of data being produced and consumed. It must then store these events in a durable manner so that downstream components can process them.

Figure 2-8 shows where a streaming data platform fits in the architecture.

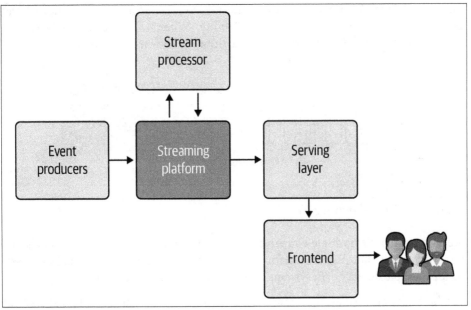

Figure 2-8. Streaming data platform

Streaming data platforms employ the concept of *topics*, which group related events together. A typical application will use more than one topic, as shown in Figure 2-9.

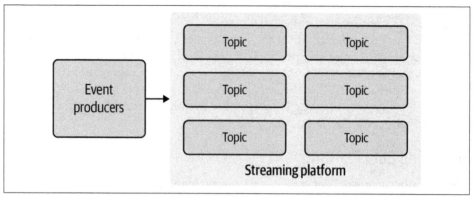

Figure 2-9. Topics in the streaming data platform

For example, we might have an `orders` topic to group related orders and a `sensory-readings` topic to group sensory readings coming from IoT devices.

Topics are backed by a distributed append-only log file. This log is partitioned and replicated across multiple nodes for reliability. When a new event arrives, it is appended to the end of the log file for its partition, as shown in Figure 2-10.

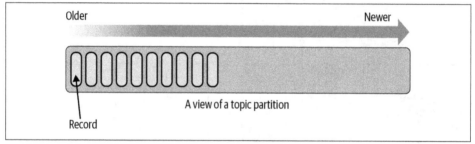

Figure 2-10. Append-only log file

Topics must handle multiple concurrent producers and consumers. It should also be possible to have multiple consumers read from the same topic, which makes it possible for multiple downstream systems to be attached to the same topic.

Apache Kafka and Amazon Kinesis were the initial front-runners in this space, but there are now other contenders like Redpanda, Apache Pulsar, and Google Pub/Sub. So how do you decide which streaming data platform to use?

The first thing to ensure is that the platform can meet your data volume and concurrency requirements. Public benchmarks are available, but we suggest that you create your own benchmark based on your data.

Once you're satisfied with that, you might want to look at the integrations available for that platform and its general ecosystem, asking the following questions:

- Does it easily integrate with your event producers so that you can get data in?
- Is it easy to get data to your downstream systems?
- Will you be able to plug metrics for the platform into your monitoring tooling?

Looking beyond this, you might want to consider the support and community available around the product to work out whether you'll be able to get help if you get stuck.

Finally, you'll want to take a look at deployment options. If you're going to deploy it yourself, will it easily fit into your existing infrastructure? And if not, is a suitable software-as-a-service (SaaS) offering available?

Stream Processing Layer

The next layer is the *stream processor*, which reads events from the streaming data platform and then takes some action on that event. Stream processors consume data from one or more topics and then run each event through a function. These functions could be written in a programming language or might be a SQL transformation.

The output of calling the function will then be written to a sink system, such as a different topic in the streaming data platform or even another database. Alternatively, the stream processor might trigger a side effect, such as sending an email or Slack notification. See Figure 2-11.

If the events in the data streaming platform are already in the shape required by the serving layer, a stream processor may not be required.

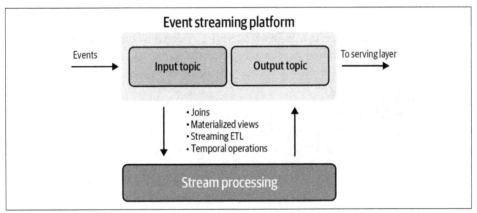

Figure 2-11. Stream processing layer

There are three patterns of stream processors use, as shown in Figure 2-12.

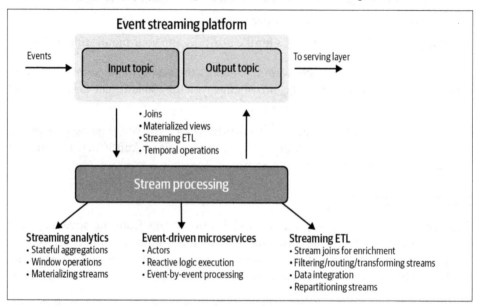

Figure 2-12. Stream processor patterns

Let's go through these patterns in turn:

Streaming analytics

Streaming analytics is all about applying a series of calculations to an incoming stream. We can do aggregate operations like counting and finding the maximum, minimum, or average. The output of these operations is usually kept in memory by the stream processor, but it may also be stored in a fault-tolerant way, so that the stream processor can recover from failures more quickly.

Event-driven microservices

Event-driven microservices is an architectural pattern where microservices inter-act with each other based on the initial consumption of events. This technique reduces latency and is used in use cases like fraud detection.

Streaming ETL

Streaming ETL plays a crucial role in building real-time data pipelines. We write individual functions and chain them together to achieve something meaningful at the end. Events pass through the pipeline, and we can do stateless operations like filtering, routing, or mapping events in whatever way we choose. We can also do stateful operations like joining streams together with windowing technologies or enriching a stream by joining it with a static dataset.

In the context of real-time analytics, stream processors are primarily used for streaming ETL and streaming analytics.

Compared to the streaming data platform, the stream processing technical landscape is quite crowded, There are traditional JVM-based stream processing engines like Flink, Spark Structured Streaming, Apache Beam, and Kafka Streams, to name just a few. But we also now have some Python-based tools like Bytewax, Faust, and Quix. By the time you read this, there will undoubtedly be even more tools in this space.

How do you decide which stream processor to use? The first criterion when working out which stream processor to use is deciding whether you need support for stateful processing. If you're only doing stateless processing, you can take your pick of the tools, but a much smaller subset support stateful operations.

Once you've decided on that, have a look at the languages supported by the stream processor. Some of them will require you to use a programming language like Java or Python, but many of the modern tools support SQL as a first-class citizen.

As with the stream processing platform, make sure that you benchmark your tool of choice to make sure that it can support your scalability and latency requirements.

Serving Layer

The *serving layer* is the primary access point for consuming real-time analytics produced in the event streaming platform. It could be a key-value store (e.g., a NoSQL database) or a real-time OLAP database, depending on your requirements. The serving layer will be accessed by real-time dashboards, data applications, recommendations engines, and used for ad hoc exploration.

But why do we need the serving layer in the first place? Can't we just serve data downstream using the event streaming platform and stream processor?

To understand the need for the serving layer, it's helpful to consider the value of events over time. The business value of individual events reduces over time, as seen in Figure 2-13.

Let's take a single event that gets captured digitally. For example, imagine someone searches for the term "pizza" in a delivery app. What is the value of knowing everything about that single event?

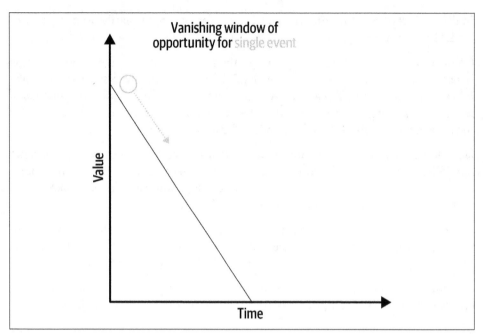

Figure 2-13. The diminishing value of individual data points over time

When it first happens, the event has a high value: It's signaling that someone, somewhere is actively searching for a pizza. If you know that is happening, you can offer coupons for establishments that happen to sell pizza.

The value of this information drops off very quickly, however. It's no use knowing that someone wanted pizza yesterday or even a few hours ago. By the time you discover this fact, the chances are that the person already bought and enjoyed a pizza from a competitor.

Conversely, the value of aggregated events increases as time passes, as shown in Figure 2-14.

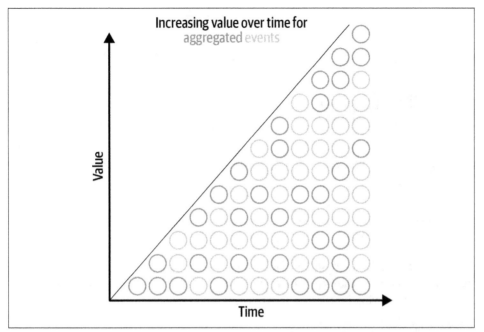

Figure 2-14. The increasing value of collective data points over time

Imagine that instead of considering a single person searching for nearby pizza, we are interested in all the people who searched for pizza within an area over time. By looking at the aggregate data, we can learn new things. We can search for trends and do some forecasting of future demand, which could help with inventory management.

Aggregate data has the opposite pattern to single-event data: it might not be precious in terms of any one event, but its value increases dramatically over time as it allows for better and better forecasts.

Making sense of aggregated events is where the serving layer (see Figure 2-15) adds value in the real-time analytics stack.

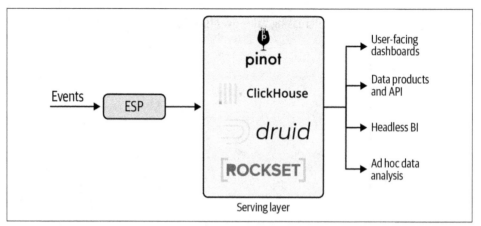

Figure 2-15. Serving layer

The serving layer is exposed to both internal and external audiences, including human users and software appliances, looking for fast and accurate analytics at scale. Therefore, the serving layer must deliver the following:

Ingestion latency
The data ingestion process needs to be really, really fast. As soon as any changes happen, you should see this reflected in the serving layer.

Query latency
After you pull in this data, you need to make sure that it can be queried as quickly as possible. We should we able to query the data in web page response times—milliseconds rather than seconds.

Concurrency
The serving layer must handle a large number of queries run at the same time. It's not uncommon for the serving layer to process hundreds of thousands of queries per second. A side effect of being able to run queries on fresh data at scale is that we'll come up with new use cases for the data. These use cases may lead to increased interaction from users and could even open more avenues for monetizing the data that we've already collected.

There are a variety of available serving layers. Key-value stores/NoSQL databases like MongoDB, Elasticsearch, and Redis are popular options. In the real-time OLAP database space, you have Apache Pinot, Apache Druid, Rockset, and ClickHouse.

How do you decide which serving layer to use? The first thing to consider is the types of queries you are likely to be running against the serving layer. If you're mostly doing key-based lookups (for example, to get the latest value by ID), then you can probably get away with using a key-value store. On the other hand, if you want to slice and dice the data across multiple dimensions, a real-time OLAP database might be a better fit. We'll assume that you're using a real-time OLAP database for the rest of this section.

The next thing to consider is how easy it is to ingest data:

- Is this done via an API or can it be done in plain SQL?
- Which of the streaming platforms are supported as data sources? Is the streaming platform that you want to use supported?
- How high is the latency from when an event appears in the streaming platform to the point at which it can be queried?
- Can the database handle the amount and rate of data being produced?

Once the data is ingested, we'll turn our attention to data storage and querying. We need to know whether our common queries respond quickly enough, and, if not, whether there's a way that we can rectify that, perhaps by adding indexes or applying pre-aggregation.

Vendors will often produce benchmarks showing how fast their technology is at ingesting and querying data. We'd suggest that you do your own testing to make sure that it meets your performance requirements.

Frontend

If the users are internal, we might be able to get away with having them query data directly from the serving layer. But if they're external, we'll definitely need a frontend for them to interact with.

There are several approaches to building a frontend:

Custom built
> If we want absolute control over the look and feel of the front end, we'll want to code it ourselves. There are a myriad of tools that make it easy to build data-intensive single-page apps (SPA), and new ones are coming out all the time.
>
> Our favorite tool for building SPAs is React.js, but there are plenty of others, including Angular.js, Ember.js, Backbone.js, Meteor.js, Polymer.js, and Vue.js.

Low-code frameworks
> Low-code frameworks reduce the amount of code that needs to be written to build an interactive web application. These platforms range from ones that let the user build an application through a graphical user interface to ones that let developers code UIs without having to learn any frontend technologies.
>
> Two of our favorite low-code frameworks are Streamlit and Plotly Dash, both of which let you build interactive frontend applications using only Python. Streamlit is an open source Python library that makes it easy to create and share

beautiful custom web apps for machine learning and data science. Dash provides similar functionality to Streamlit and is built on top of Plotly, React, and Flask.

Data visualization

Data visualization tools provide drag-and-drop functionality for generating dashboards. These tools make it easy to populate different types of charts and don't require any coding at all. They are less powerful than low-code frameworks but easier to use.

Our favorite data visualization tools are Superset and Redash, but there are others, including Grafana, Retool, and Metabase.

How do you know which one to use? You'll need to consider the following criteria:

Frontend coding experience

Do you have software engineers that are experience with the frontend stack, such that they could build an interactive UI?

Time

How much time do you have to get the get the front end ready? If you're short for time, it might make sense to use a framework that's already done some of the heavy lifting.

Internal or external

Are the users of the frontend internal to your organization or not? If they are internal, a data visualization or low-code option might make more sense.

Summary

This chapter described the types of components that form the real-time analytics stack, as well as covering some of the technologies that fit in each category. One thing to keep in mind is that technologies blur the lines between categories and don't fit completely cleanly into one category. For example, Apache Pulsar, a data streaming platform, supports functions that let you transform data from one stream and write out to another stream, which would usually be the job of a stream processor.

In the next chapters, we're going to learn how to use these components to build a real-time application.

CHAPTER 3

Introducing All About That Dough: Real-Time Analytics on Pizza

In this chapter we'll introduce a pizza delivery service called All About That Dough (AATD) that specializes in pizzas with Indian toppings. It's been operating for almost two decades and has built up an infrastructure that allows the company to serve thousands of page views per minute on its websites, with a peak of 50 orders per minute.

AATD deals with three types of data: products, users, and orders. When it started out, the company used a relational database to store all this data, but a couple of years ago it introduced a streaming platform to deal with orders.

Every hour the data processed by the streaming platform is batched up before being loaded into a data warehouse, where analytical queries are run each night to see what's happened in the business that day. AATD also store access logs of all visits to the website but so far hasn't done anything with this data.

While AATD has done reasonably well at growing its business, several recurring problems are prohibiting further improvement:

- The company sometimes receives fraudulent or prank orders but doesn't realize it until order processing has begun or even sometimes until days after the orders have been processed.

- Inventory management is difficult because the company doesn't have a good idea of which products are popular at any particular moment. On multiple occasions, the company ran out of ingredients because of a surge in particular lines of pizzas.

- Users often complain that they don't know when their orders are going to arrive, and they want transparency with respect to the progress of their order.

AATD's management team has called us in as consultants to advise them on changes that can be made to their application's architecture to solve some (or all) of these problems. They are open to trying out new technologies but would prefer it if we use open source technologies in our solution so that they aren't completely locked into any one vendor.

Existing Architecture

Let's start by looking at AATD's existing data infrastructure, shown in Figure 3-1.

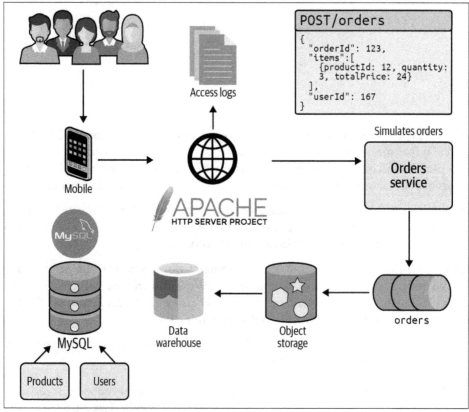

Figure 3-1. AATD's existing architecture

We've included the object storage and data warehouse in the diagram, but those are out of scope for the purpose of this book. AATD can continue to use its existing data warehouse solution for its historical data analysis needs.

Let's go through the other parts of the architecture, starting with users making requests to the web server, as highlighted in Figure 3-2.

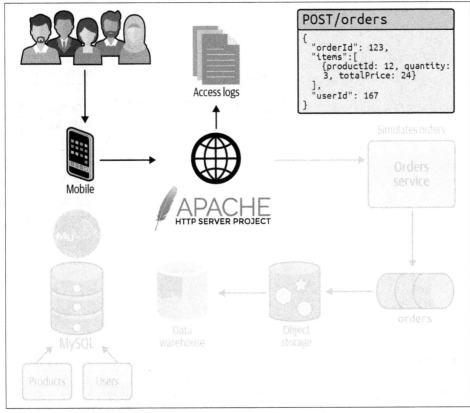

Figure 3-2. The user makes a web request

Users access AATD's website on their mobile phones, and all page requests are recorded into access log files. If the user makes an order, a POST request will be sent containing the details of the order.

The order is then sent to the orders service, as shown in Figure 3-3, which applies some validation logic and then appends the order to the event streaming platform.

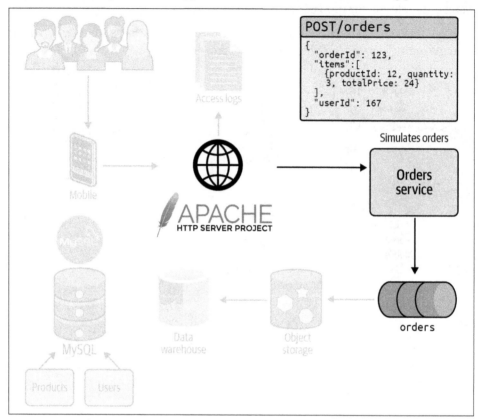

Figure 3-3. Orders are sent to the orders service

Finally, we have a MySQL database, as shown in Figure 3-4, that acts as the system of record for users and products.

This data is used by backend services in AATD that are aren't included in their analytics infrastructure, and are therefore out of the scope of this book.

In the next section, you'll learn how to get AATD's existing architecture set up on your machine.

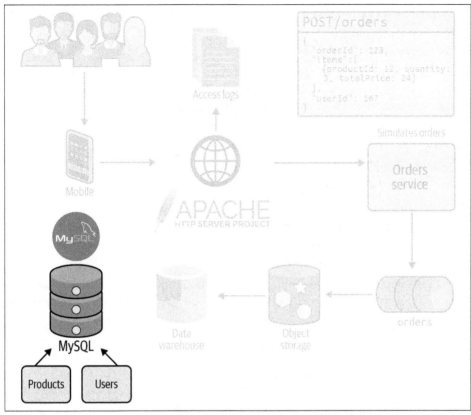

Figure 3-4. Users and products are stored in MySQL

Setup

This book has a companion GitHub repository (*https://oreil.ly/RTA-github*) that contains all the code used in each of the chapters. If you're a Git user, you can clone the repository locally by running the following command:

```
git clone git@github.com:mneedham/real-time-analytics-book.git
cd real-time-analytics-book
```

If you aren't a Git user, you can still download a ZIP file that contains all the samples:

```
wget github.com/mneedham/real-time-analytics-book/archive/refs/heads/main.zip
unzip main.zip
```

We're going to be using Docker to run all the components of our application. The Docker Compose files are available in the root directory of the repository and have a docker-compose prefix. Let's go through each of the components.

MySQL

MySQL is a popular and widely used open source relational database management system that has been around since 1995. It is known for its ease of use, robustness, and reliability.

It stores data in tables (or relations) that can be connected to each other by primary keys and foreign keys. Tables can be joined at query time via these keys. Querying is done using SQL, the standard language for managing relational databases.

MySQL is a popular choice for a range of applications and use cases, from small-scale projects to large-scale enterprise systems. We'll be using it to store products and users.

The service configuration is shown in Example 3-1.

Example 3-1. docker-compose-base.yml—MySQL

```
mysql:
  image: mysql/mysql-server:8.0.27
  hostname: mysql
  container_name: mysql
  ports:
    - 3306:3306
  environment:
    - MYSQL_ROOT_PASSWORD=debezium
    - MYSQL_USER=mysqluser
    - MYSQL_PASSWORD=mysqlpw
  volumes:
    - ${PWD}/mysql/mysql.cnf:/etc/mysql/conf.d
    - ${PWD}/mysql/mysql_boots.sql:/docker-entrypoint-initdb.d/mysql_bootstrap.sql
    - ${PWD}/mysql/data:/var/lib/mysql-files/data
```

The schema for the database is shown in Figure 3-5.

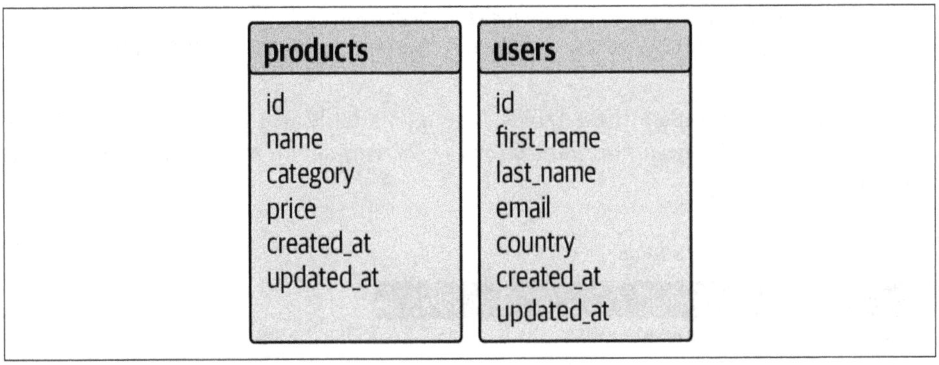

Figure 3-5. MySQL schema

The SQL to create these tables is included in the bootstrap file (*/docker-entrypoint-initdb.d/mysql_bootstrap.sql*) that is run when the container is created. Let's take a closer look at the contents of the bootstrap file.

First, we create the database `pizzashop` if it doesn't already exist and give permissions to the `mysqluser`:

```
CREATE DATABASE IF NOT EXISTS pizzashop;
USE pizzashop;

GRANT ALL PRIVILEGES ON pizzashop.* TO 'mysqluser';
GRANT FILE on *.* to 'mysqluser';
FLUSH PRIVILEGES;
```

Next, create the `users` table:

```
CREATE TABLE IF NOT EXISTS pizzashop.users
(
    id SERIAL PRIMARY KEY,
    first_name VARCHAR(255),
    last_name VARCHAR(255),
    email VARCHAR(255),
    country VARCHAR(255),
    created_at TIMESTAMP DEFAULT CURRENT_TIMESTAMP,
    updated_at DATETIME DEFAULT CURRENT_TIMESTAMP ON UPDATE CURRENT_TIMESTAMP
);
```

And the `products` table:

```
CREATE TABLE IF NOT EXISTS pizzashop.products
(
    id SERIAL PRIMARY KEY,
    name VARCHAR(100),
    description VARCHAR(500),
    category VARCHAR(100),
    price FLOAT,
    image VARCHAR(200),
```

```
    created_at TIMESTAMP DEFAULT CURRENT_TIMESTAMP,
    updated_at DATETIME DEFAULT CURRENT_TIMESTAMP ON UPDATE CURRENT_TIMESTAMP
);
```

And, finally, we'll populate these tables. The users table will be populated with the contents of */var/lib/mysql-files/data/users.csv*, a sample of which can be seen in Table 3-1.

Table 3-1. Sample of users table

firstName	lastName	email	country
Waldo	Morteo	wmorteo0@toplist.cz	Benin
Anselm	Tabbernor	atabbernor1@biglobe.ne.jp	Ukraine
Jane	Razoux	jrazoux2@webnode.com	Ukraine
Xavier	Adamski	xadamski3@free.fr	Indonesia
Adan	Griffith	agriffith4@rambler.ru	Indonesia
Lea	Queenborough	lqueenborough5@toplist.cz	United States
Diandra	Nadin	dnadin6@cnet.com	Kazakhstan
Dareen	Connue	dconnue7@blogtalkradio.com	Indonesia

The code to import the users is as follows:

```
LOAD DATA INFILE '/var/lib/mysql-files/data/users.csv'
INTO TABLE pizzashop.users
FIELDS TERMINATED BY ','
OPTIONALLY ENCLOSED BY '"'
IGNORE 1 LINES
(first_name,last_name,email,country);
```

The products table will be populated with the contents of */var/lib/mysql-files/data/products.csv*, a sample of which can be seen in Table 3-2.

Table 3-2. Sample of products table

name	description	price	category	image
Moroccan Spice Pasta Pizza - Veg	A pizza loaded with a spicy combination of Harissa sauce and delicious pasta	335.0	veg pizzas	https://oreil.ly/LCGSv
Pepsi (500ml)		60.0	beverages	https://oreil.ly/pJYwR
Pepsi Black Can	PEPSI BLACK CAN	60.0	beverages	https://oreil.ly/nYCzO
Tikka Masala Pasta Veg		129.0	pasta	https://oreil.ly/KbRY7

The code to import the products is as follows:

```
LOAD DATA INFILE '/var/lib/mysql-files/data/products.csv'
INTO TABLE pizzashop.products
FIELDS TERMINATED BY ','
OPTIONALLY ENCLOSED BY '"'
```

```
IGNORE 1 LINES
(name,description,price,category,image);
```

Apache Kafka

Apache Kafka is our event streaming platform and is widely used by organizations to handle large volumes of real-time data. It is designed to enable high-throughput, low-latency processing of data streams, making it a popular choice for applications that require fast and reliable data processing.

Kafka's distributed architecture offers support for multiple data producers and consumers, enabling the creation of complex and scalable data pipelines. In addition, Kafka Connect makes it easy to integrate with a wide range of systems and applications. Kafka is probably the most popular solution for building modern, data-driven applications.

Orders from the website are published to Kafka via the orders service. The configuration for this service is shown in Example 3-2.

Example 3-2. docker-compose-base.yml—Kafka

```
kafka:
  image: confluentinc/cp-kafka:7.1.0
  hostname: kafka
  container_name: kafka
  ports:
    - "29092:29092"
  environment:
    KAFKA_BROKER_ID: 1
    KAFKA_ZOOKEEPER_CONNECT: 'zookeeper:2181'
    KAFKA_LISTENER_SECURITY_PROTOCOL_MAP:
      PLAINTEXT:PLAINTEXT,PLAINTEXT_HOST:PLAINTEXT
    KAFKA_ADVERTISED_LISTENERS:
      PLAINTEXT://kafka:9092,PLAINTEXT_HOST://localhost:29092
    KAFKA_OFFSETS_TOPIC_REPLICATION_FACTOR: 1
    KAFKA_GROUP_INITIAL_REBALANCE_DELAY_MS: 0
    KAFKA_TOOLS_LOG4J_LOGLEVEL: ERROR
  depends_on:
    [zookeeper]
```

ZooKeeper

Apache ZooKeeper is a distributed coordination service that is a core component of many distributed systems. It provides a highly available hierarchical key-value store that can be used to store configuration data, manage leadership election, act as a message queue, and more.

Its robust and reliable infrastructure means that ZooKeeper provides a solid foundation for building scalable distributed systems. We'll be using it to track the status of nodes in the Kafka cluster and maintain a list of Kafka topics and messages.

The configuration for this service is shown in Example 3-3.

Example 3-3. docker-compose-base.yml—ZooKeeper

```
zookeeper:
  image: zookeeper:latest
  hostname: zookeeper
  container_name: zookeeper
  ports:
    - "2181:2181"
  environment:
    ZOO_MY_ID: 1
    ZOO_PORT: 2181
    ZOO_SERVERS: server.1=zookeeper:2888:3888;2181
```

Orders Service

The *orders service* publishes multiple orders per second into the orders topic in Kafka. The structure of the events in this topic is shown here:

```
{
    "id":"string",
    "createdAt":"string",
    "userId":"integer",
    "price":"double",
    "status":"string",
    "items": [
        {
            "productId": "string",
            "quantity": "integer",
            "price": double
        }
    ]
}
```

The configuration for this service is shown in Example 3-4.

Example 3-4. docker-compose-base.yml—orders service

```
orders-service:
  build: orders-service
  container_name: orders-service
  depends_on:
    - mysql
    - kafka
```

This is a custom Docker image that contains a data simulator. We won't go into detail about the data simulator in the book, but you can find the simulator code (*https://oreil.ly/z5YIL*) in the book's GitHub repository.

Spinning Up the Components

You can launch all these components by running the following command:

```
docker-compose -f docker-compose-base.yml up
```

Once we've done this, we'll have instances of Kafka, MySQL, and ZooKeeper running. The orders service will be running as well and will have populated Kafka with order data, and MySQL with user and product data.

Inspecting the Data

Let's have a look at a subset of AATD's data, starting with the MySQL tables. We can connect to MySQL using the CLI, as shown in the following command:

```
docker exec -it mysql mysql -u mysqluser -p
```

Enter the password **mysqlpw**, and then you'll see the mysql prompt:

```
Welcome to the MySQL monitor.  Commands end with ; or \g.
Your MySQL connection id is 5902
Server version: 8.0.27 MySQL Community Server - GPL

Copyright (c) 2000, 2021, Oracle and/or its affiliates.

Oracle is a registered trademark of Oracle Corporation and/or its
affiliates. Other names may be trademarks of their respective owners.

Type 'help;' or '\h' for help. Type '\c' to clear the current input statement.

mysql>
```

We can query the products table with the following query:

```
SELECT count(*)
FROM pizzashop.products;
```

The results of running this query are shown in Table 3-3.

Table 3-3. Count of products

count(*)
81

We have 81 different products. Let's have a look at some of them:

```
SELECT name, description, category, price
FROM pizzashop.products
LIMIT 10;
```

The results of running this query are shown in Table 3-4.

Table 3-4. First 10 products

name	description	category	price
Moroccan Spice Pasta Pizza - Veg	A pizza loaded with a spicy combination of Harissa sauce and delicious pasta	veg pizzas	335
Pepsi (500ml)		beverages	60
Pepsi Black Can	PEPSI BLACK CAN	beverages	60
Tikka Masala Pasta Veg		pasta	129
Veggie Paradise	Golden Corn, Black Olives, Capsicum & Red Paprika	veg pizzas	385
Lipton Ice Tea (250ml)		beverages	50
The 4 Cheese Pizza	Cheese Overloaded pizza with 4 different varieties of cheese and 4 times the cheese of a normal pizza, including a spicy hit of Ghost	veg pizzas	649
Chicken Pepperoni	A classic American taste! Relish the delectable flavor of Chicken Pepperoni, topped with extra cheese	non veg pizzas	365
Stuffed Garlic Bread	Freshly Baked Garlic Bread stuffed with mozzarella cheese, sweet corn, & tangy and spicy jalapeños	side orders	139
Cheese Dip	A dreamy creamy cheese dip to add that extra tang to your snack	side orders	25

We can write a similar query to return users:

```
SELECT id, first_name, last_name, email, country
FROM pizzashop.users
LIMIT 10;
```

The results of running this query are shown in Table 3-5.

Table 3-5. First 10 users

id	first_name	last_name	email	country
1	Waldo	Morteo	wmorteo0@toplist.cz	Benin
2	Anselm	Tabbernor	atabbernor1@biglobe.ne.jp	Ukraine
3	Jane	Razoux	jrazoux2@webnode.com	Ukraine
4	Xavier	Adamski	xadamski3@free.fr	Indonesia
5	Adan	Griffith	agriffith4@rambler.ru	Indonesia
6	Lea	Queenborough	lqueenborough5@toplist.cz	United States
7	Diandra	Nadin	dnadin6@cnet.com	Kazakhstan
8	Dareen	Connue	dconnue7@blogtalkradio.com	Indonesia
9	Bab	Audibert	baudibert8@google.cn	Albania
10	Issie	Hargrave	ihargrave9@ehow.com	Russia

That data has all loaded correctly.

 If you don't see any records when running these queries, an error likely occurred during the import process. Look at the Docker logs for any error messages that may help diagnose the problem.

Let's now have a look at the data in Apache Kafka. We can do this using the kcat command-line utility (*https://oreil.ly/hb-9y*), described by the Confluent documentation as follows:

> kcat is a command-line utility that you can use to test and debug Apache Kafka deployments. You can use kcat to produce, consume, and list topic and partition information for Kafka. Described as "netcat for Kafka," it is a Swiss Army knife of tools for inspecting and creating data in Kafka.

Call kcat with the following arguments:

```
kcat -C -b localhost:29092 -t orders -c 1
```

By default this command will keep returning events as long as they are being produced, but we'll restrict it to just a single message for brevity's sake. If we run this command, you'll see output that looks like Example 3-5.

Example 3-5. A message in the `orders` stream

```
{
  "id": "c6745d1f-cecb-4aa8-993b-6dea64d06f52",
  "createdAt": "2022-09-06T10:46:17.703283",
  "userId": 416,
  "status": "PLACED_ORDER",
  "price": 1040,
  "items": [
    {
      "productId": "21",
      "quantity": 2,
      "price": 45
    },
    {
      "productId": "36",
      "quantity": 3,
      "price": 60
    },
    {
      "productId": "72",
      "quantity": 2,
      "price": 385
    }
```

```
    ]
}
```

It looks like the orders are streaming as expected. We can see that the structure of an event contains an event ID, a user ID, the status of the order, the time it was placed, and then an array that contains the order items.

 If there aren't any events in the `orders` topic, this command will hang, and nothing will be printed to the terminal. This indicates an issue with the orders service, which you'll need to debug by looking at the Docker logs.

In summary, we've now walked through all the components of AATD's existing architecture that we'll be interacting with. You can see a diagram of everything in Figure 3-6.

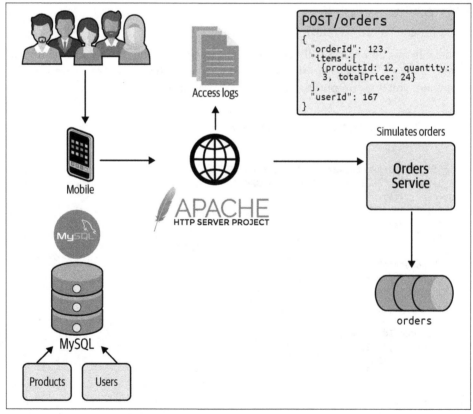

Figure 3-6. Existing architecture

Now that we've got the existing architecture configured, it's time to think about how we're going to implement real-time analytics applications based on this data.

Applications of Real-Time Analytics

Let's go through the ways that we could introduce real-time analytics functionality. AATD will act as an example of a business that can implement real-time analytics in the quadrants we saw in "Classifying Real-Time Analytics Applications" on page 9.

The following are some potential applications that we could build to solve various business problems for AATD:

Human-based/internal
A *dashboard* showing the latest orders, revenue, products ordered, and customer satisfaction. This will allow AATD's operators to keep on top of what's currently happening with the business and react to problems as they happen.

Human-based/external
A *web/mobile application* that lets customers track order status and the time until their pizza gets delivered on a live map. This will allow AATD's users to plan for the arrival of their order and get an early indication if anything is going wrong with the order.

Machine-based/internal
An *anomaly detection system* on AATD's access logs that sends alerts via Slack or email when unusual traffic patterns are detected. This will allow AATD's site reliability engineering (SRE) team to make sure the website is highly available and to detect denial-of-service attacks.

Machine-based/external
A *fraud detection system* that detects and blocks fraudulent orders.

We are going to focus on the human-based applications in this book, but we'll leave the machine-based ones as an exercise for the reader!

Summary

In this chapter, we introduced All About That Dough, a pizza chain that wants to use real-time analytics to improve its business. We learned about AATD's existing architecture and got it set up on our machine.

In the next four chapters, we'll build on top of this architecture, adding additional components for each of the four types of real-time analytics applications introduced in "Classifying Real-Time Analytics Applications" on page 9. In the next chapter, we'll start with an internal dashboard that will be used to keep track of orders being placed.

CHAPTER 4

Querying Kafka with Kafka Streams

AATD doesn't currently have real-time insight into the number of orders being placed or the revenue being generated. The company would like to know if there are spikes or dips in the numbers of orders so that it can react more quickly in the operations part of the business.

The AATD engineering team is already familiar with Kafka Streams from other applications that they've built, so we're going to create a Kafka Streams app that exposes an HTTP endpoint showing recent orders and revenue. We'll build this app with the Quarkus framework, starting with a naive version. Then we'll apply some optimizations. We'll conclude with a summary of the limitations of using a stream processor to query streaming data. Figure 4-1 shows what we'll be building in this chapter.

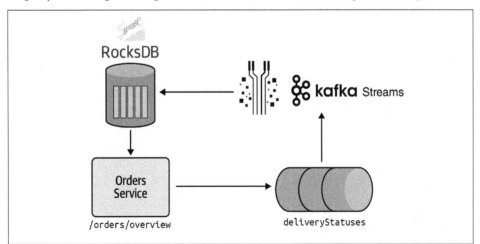

Figure 4-1. Kafka Streams architecture

What Is Kafka Streams?

Kafka Streams (*https://oreil.ly/vjT2-*) is a library for building streaming applications that transform input Kafka topics into output Kafka topics. It is an example of the stream processor component of the real-time analytics stack described in Chapter 2.

Kafka Streams is often used for joining, filtering, and transforming streams, but in this chapter we're going to use it to query an existing stream.

At the heart of a Kafka Streams application is a *topology*, which defines the stream processing logic of the application. A topology describes how data is consumed from input streams (source) and then transformed into something that can be produced to output streams (sink).

More specifically, Jacek Laskowski, author of *The Internals of Kafka Streams* (*https://oreil.ly/Ozl_N*), defines a topology as follows:

> A directed acyclic graph of stream processing nodes that represents the stream processing logic of a Kafka Streams application.

In this graph, the nodes are the processing work, and the relationships are streams. Through this topology, we can create powerful streaming applications that can handle even the most complex data processing tasks. You can see an example topology in Figure 4-2.

Kafka Streams provides a domain-specific language (DSL) that simplifies the building of these topologies.

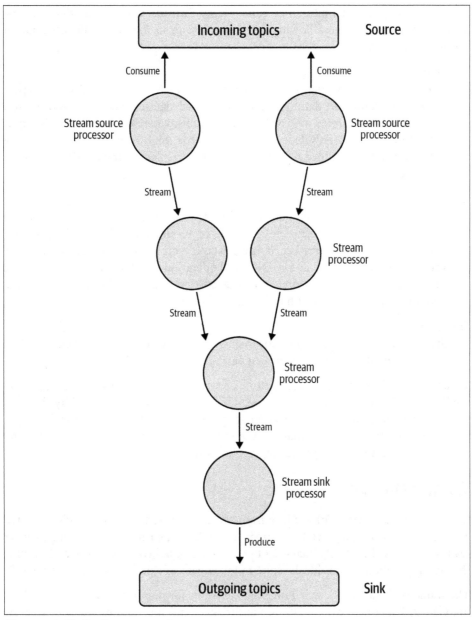

Figure 4-2. Kafka Streams topology

Let's go through the definitions of some Kafka Streams abstractions that we'll be using in this section. The following definitions are from the official documentation (*https://oreil.ly/9JXr3*):

KStream

A KStream is an abstraction of a record stream, where each data record represents a self-contained datum in the unbounded dataset. The data records in a KStream are interpreted as "INSERT" operations, where each record adds a new entry to an append-only ledger. In other words, each record represents a new piece of data that is added to the stream without replacing any existing data with the same key.

KTable

A KTable is an abstraction of a change log stream, where each data record represents an update. Each record in a KTable represents an update to the previous value for a specific record key, if any exists. If a corresponding key doesn't exist yet, the update is treated as an "INSERT" operation. In other words, each record in a KTable represents an update to the existing data with the same key or the addition of a new record with a new key-value pair.

State Store

State Stores are storage engines for managing the state of stream processors. They can store the state in memory or in a database like RocksDB.

When stateful functions like aggregation or windowing functions are called, intermediate data is stored in the State Store. This data can then be queried by the read side of a stream processing application to generate output streams or tables. State Stores are an efficient way to manage the state of stream processors and enable the creation of powerful stream processing applications in Kafka Streams.

What Is Quarkus?

Quarkus (*https://quarkus.io*) is a Java framework optimized for building cloud native applications that are deployed on Kubernetes. Developed by Red Hat's engineering team and released in 2019, Quarkus offers a modern, lightweight approach to building Java applications that is ideally suited to the needs of cloud native development.

The framework includes a wide range of extensions for popular technologies, including Camel, Hibernate, MongoDB, Kafka Streams, and more. These extensions provide a simple and efficient way to integrate these tools into your microservices architecture, speeding up development time and streamlining the process of building complex distributed systems.

The native Kafka Streams integration in particular makes it a great choice for us (*https://oreil.ly/6nPcZ*).

Quarkus Application

Now that we've got the definitions out of the way, it's time to start building our Kafka Streams app.

Installing the Quarkus CLI

The Quarkus CLI is a powerful tool that lets us create and manage Quarkus applications from the command line. With the Quarkus CLI, we can quickly scaffold new applications, generate code, run tests, and deploy our applications to various environments There are many ways to install the CLI, so you can almost certainly find one that you prefer.

I'm a big fan of SDKMAN (*https://sdkman.io*), so I'm going to install it using that. SDKMAN makes it easy to install and manage software development kits (SDKs). It has lots of useful features, including automated updates, environment management, and support for multiple platforms. I use it to run different Java versions on my machine.

We can install Quarkus with SDKMAN by running the following command:

```
sdk install quarkus
```

We can check that it's installed by running the following command:

```
quarkus --version
```

You should see output similar to Example 4-1.

Example 4-1. Quarkus version

```
2.13.1.Final
```

 The Quarkus CLI isn't mandatory, but having it installed does make the development process much smoother, so we suggest installing it!

Creating a Quarkus Application

Now that we've got that installed, we can run the following command to create our pizza shop app:

```
quarkus create app pizzashop --package-name pizzashop
cd pizzashop
```

This command will create a Maven application with most of the dependencies that we'll need and a skeleton structure to get us started. The only thing missing is Kafka Streams, which we can add using the `kafka-streams` extension:

```
quarkus extension add 'kafka-streams'
```

We're now ready to start building our application.

Creating a Topology

The first thing we need to do is create a Kafka Streams topology. A Quarkus application can define a single topology, in which we'll define all our stream operations. This could include joining streams together to create a new stream, filtering a stream, creating a key-value store based on a stream, and more.

Once we have our topology class, we'll create a couple of window stores that keep track of the total orders and revenue generated in the last couple of minutes. This will allow us to create an HTTP endpoint that returns a summary of the latest orders based on the contents of these stores.

Create the file *src/main/java/pizzashop/streams/Topology.java* and add this:

```java
package pizzashop.streams;

import org.apache.kafka.common.serialization.Serde;
import org.apache.kafka.common.serialization.Serdes;
import org.apache.kafka.common.utils.Bytes;
import org.apache.kafka.streams.StreamsBuilder;
import org.apache.kafka.streams.kstream.*;
import org.apache.kafka.streams.state.WindowStore;
import pizzashop.deser.JsonDeserializer;
import pizzashop.deser.JsonSerializer;
import pizzashop.models.Order;

import javax.enterprise.context.ApplicationScoped;
import javax.enterprise.inject.Produces;
import java.time.Duration;

@ApplicationScoped
public class Topology {
    @Produces
    public org.apache.kafka.streams.Topology buildTopology() {
        final Serde<Order> orderSerde = Serdes.serdeFrom(new JsonSerializer<>(),
            new JsonDeserializer<>(Order.class));

        // Create a stream over the `orders` topic
        StreamsBuilder builder = new StreamsBuilder();
        KStream<String, Order> orders = builder.stream("orders",
            Consumed.with(Serdes.String(), orderSerde));

        // Defining the window size of our state store
```

```
Duration windowSize = Duration.ofSeconds(60);
Duration advanceSize = Duration.ofSeconds(1);
Duration gracePeriod = Duration.ofSeconds(60);
TimeWindows timeWindow = TimeWindows.ofSizeAndGrace(
    windowSize, gracePeriod).advanceBy(advanceSize);

// Create an OrdersCountStore that keeps track of the
// number of orders over the last two minutes
orders.groupBy(
        (key, value) -> "count",
        Grouped.with(Serdes.String(), orderSerde))
        .windowedBy(timeWindow)
        .count(Materialized.as("OrdersCountStore")
);

// Create a RevenueStore that keeps track of the amount of revenue
// generated over the last two minutes
orders.groupBy(
        (key, value) -> "count",
        Grouped.with(Serdes.String(), orderSerde))
        .windowedBy(timeWindow)
        .aggregate(
            () -> 0.0,
            (key, value, aggregate) -> aggregate + value.price,
            Materialized.
                <String, Double, WindowStore<Bytes, byte[]>>
                as("RevenueStore")
                .withValueSerde(Serdes.Double())
        );

    return builder.build();
    }
}
```

In this code, we first create a KStream based on the `orders` topic, before creating the `OrdersCountStore` and `RevenueStore`, which store a one-minute rolling window of the number of orders and revenue generated. The grace period is usually used to capture late-arriving events, but we're using it so that we have two minutes' worth of windows kept around, which we'll need later on.

We also have the following model classes that represent events in the `orders` stream:

```
package pizzashop.models;

import io.quarkus.runtime.annotations.RegisterForReflection;
import java.util.List;

@RegisterForReflection
public class Order {
    public Order() { }

    public String id;
```

```
    public String userId;
    public String createdAt;
    public double price;
    public double deliveryLat;
    public double deliveryLon;
    public List<OrderItem> items;
}

package pizzashop.models;

public class OrderItem {
    public String productId;
    public int quantity;
    public double price;
}
```

Querying the Key-Value Store

Next, we'll create the class `src/main/java/pizzashop/streams/OrdersQueries`
`.java`, which will abstract our interactions with the `OrdersStore`. The querying of
state stores (like `OrdersStore`) uses a feature of Kafka Streams called interactive
queries (*https://oreil.ly/TXzdP*):

```
package pizzashop.streams;

import org.apache.kafka.streams.KafkaStreams;
import org.apache.kafka.streams.KeyValue;
import org.apache.kafka.streams.StoreQueryParameters;
import org.apache.kafka.streams.errors.InvalidStateStoreException;
import org.apache.kafka.streams.state.*;

import pizzashop.models.*;

import javax.enterprise.context.ApplicationScoped;
import javax.inject.Inject;
import java.time.Instant;

@ApplicationScoped
public class OrdersQueries {
    @Inject
    KafkaStreams streams;

    public OrdersSummary ordersSummary() {
        KStreamsWindowStore<Long> countStore = new KStreamsWindowStore<>(
            ordersCountsStore());
        KStreamsWindowStore<Double> revenueStore = new KStreamsWindowStore<>(
            revenueStore());

        Instant now = Instant.now();
        Instant oneMinuteAgo = now.minusSeconds(60);
        Instant twoMinutesAgo = now.minusSeconds(120);
```

```
        long recentCount = countStore.firstEntry(oneMinuteAgo, now);
        double recentRevenue = revenueStore.firstEntry(oneMinuteAgo, now);

        long  previousCount = countStore.firstEntry(twoMinutesAgo, oneMinuteAgo);
        double previousRevenue = revenueStore.firstEntry(
            twoMinutesAgo, oneMinuteAgo);

        TimePeriod currentTimePeriod = new TimePeriod
          (recentCount, recentRevenue);
        TimePeriod previousTimePeriod = new TimePeriod
          (previousCount, previousRevenue);
        return new OrdersSummary(currentTimePeriod, previousTimePeriod);
    }

    private ReadOnlyWindowStore<String, Double> revenueStore() {
        while (true) {
            try {
                return streams.store(StoreQueryParameters.fromNameAndType(
                        "RevenueStore", QueryableStoreTypes.windowStore()
                ));
            } catch (InvalidStateStoreException e) {
                System.out.println("e = " + e);
            }
        }
    }

    private ReadOnlyWindowStore<String, Long> ordersCountsStore() {
        while (true) {
            try {
                return streams.store(StoreQueryParameters.fromNameAndType(
                        "OrdersCountStore", QueryableStoreTypes.windowStore()
                ));
            } catch (InvalidStateStoreException e) {
                System.out.println("e = " + e);
            }
        }
    }
}
```

Both ordersCountsStore and revenueStore are returning data from window stores
that hold the order count and amount of revenue generated, respectively. The reason
for the while(true) { try {} catch {} } code block in both functions is that the
store might not be available if we call this code before the stream thread is in a
RUNNING state. Assuming we don't have any bugs in our code, we will eventually get to
the RUNNING state; it just might take a bit longer than it takes for the HTTP endpoint
to start up.

ordersSummary calls those two functions to get the number of orders for the last
minute and the minute before that, as well as the total revenue for the last minute and
the minute before that.

`KStreamsWindowStore.java` is defined here:

```java
package pizzashop.models;

import org.apache.kafka.streams.state.ReadOnlyWindowStore;
import org.apache.kafka.streams.state.WindowStoreIterator;

import java.time.Instant;

public class KStreamsWindowStore<T> {
    private final ReadOnlyWindowStore<String, T> store;

    public KStreamsWindowStore(ReadOnlyWindowStore<String, T> store) {
        this.store = store;
    }

    public T firstEntry(Instant from, Instant to) {
        try (WindowStoreIterator<T> iterator = store.fetch("count", from, to)) {
            if (iterator.hasNext()) {
                return iterator.next().value;
            }
        }
        throw new RuntimeException(
            "No entries found in store between " + from + " and " + to);
    }
}
```

The `firstEntry` method finds the first entry in the window store in the provided date range and returns the value. If no entries, exist it will throw an error.

`OrdersSummary.java` is defined here:

```java
package pizzashop.models;

import io.quarkus.runtime.annotations.RegisterForReflection;

@RegisterForReflection
public class OrdersSummary {
    private TimePeriod currentTimePeriod;
    private TimePeriod previousTimePeriod;

    public OrdersSummary(
        TimePeriod currentTimePeriod, TimePeriod previousTimePeriod) {
        this.currentTimePeriod = currentTimePeriod;
        this.previousTimePeriod = previousTimePeriod;
    }

    public TimePeriod getCurrentTimePeriod() { return currentTimePeriod; }
    public TimePeriod getPreviousTimePeriod() { return previousTimePeriod; }
}
```

This class is a data object that keeps track of orders and revenue for the current and previous time periods.

`TimePeriod.java` is defined here:

```
package pizzashop.models;

import io.quarkus.runtime.annotations.RegisterForReflection;

@RegisterForReflection
public class TimePeriod {
    private int orders;
    private double totalPrice;

    public TimePeriod(long orders, double totalPrice) {
        this.orders = orders;
        this.totalPrice = totalPrice;
    }

    public int getOrders() { return orders; }
    public double getTotalPrice() { return totalPrice; }
}
```

This class is a data object that keeps track of orders and revenue.

Creating an HTTP Endpoint

Finally, let's create the HTTP endpoint that exposes the summary data to our users.
Create the file *src/main/java/pizzashop/rest/OrdersResource.java* and add this:

```
package pizzashop.rest;

import pizzashop.models.OrdersSummary;
import pizzashop.streams.InteractiveQueries;
import javax.enterprise.context.ApplicationScoped;
import javax.inject.Inject;
import javax.ws.rs.GET;
import javax.ws.rs.Path;
import javax.ws.rs.core.Response;

@ApplicationScoped
@Path("/orders")
public class OrdersResource {
    @Inject
    OrdersQueries ordersQueries;

    @GET
    @Path("/overview")
    public Response overview() {
        OrdersSummary ordersSummary = ordersQueries.ordersSummary();
        return Response.ok(ordersSummary).build();
    }
}
```

Running the Application

Now that we've created all our classes, it's time to run the application. We can do this by running the following command:

```
QUARKUS_KAFKA_STREAMS_BOOTSTRAP_SERVERS=localhost:29092 quarkus dev
```

We pass in the `QUARKUS_KAFKA_STREAMS_BOOTSTRAP_SERVERS` environment variable so that Quarkus can connect to our Kafka broker.

Querying the HTTP Endpoint

Now we can query the HTTP endpoint to see how many orders our online service is receiving. The endpoint is available on port 8080 at /orders/overview:

```
curl http://localhost:8080/orders/overview 2>/dev/null | jq '.'
```

The results of this command are shown in Example 4-2.

Example 4-2. Latest orders state

```json
{
  "currentTimePeriod": {
    "orders": 994,
    "totalPrice": 4496973
  },
  "previousTimePeriod": {
    "orders": 985,
    "totalPrice": 4535117
  }
}
```

Success! We can see the number of orders and the total revenue in the current and previous time periods.

Limitations of Kafka Streams

While this approach for querying streams has been successful in many cases, certain factors could impact its efficacy for our particular use case. In this section, we will take a closer look at these limitations to better understand how they could affect the performance of this approach.

The underlying database used by Kafka Streams is RocksDB, a key-value store that allows you to store and retrieve data using key-value pairs. This fork of Google's LevelDB is optimized for write-heavy workloads with large datasets.

One of its constraints is that we can create only one index per key-value store. This means that if we decide to query the data along another dimension, we'll need to update the topology to create another key-value store. If we do a non-key search, RocksDB will do a full scan to find the matching records, leading to high query latency.

Our key-value stores are also capturing only events that happened in the last one minute and the minute before that. If we wanted to capture data going further back, we'd need to update the topology to capture more events. In AATD's case, we could imagine a future use case where we'd want to compare the sales numbers from right now with the numbers from this same time last week or last month. This would be difficult to do in Kafka Streams because we'd need to store historical data, which would take up a lot of memory.

So although we can use Kafka Streams to write real-time analytics queries and it will do a reasonable job, we probably need to find a tool that better fits the problem.

Summary

In this chapter, we looked at how to build an HTTP API on top of the `orders` stream so that we can get an aggregate view of what's happening with orders in the business. We built this solution using Kafka Streams, but we realized that this might not be the most appropriate tool for the job. In the next, chapter we'll learn why we need a serving layer to build a scalable real-time analytics application.

CHAPTER 5

The Serving Layer: Apache Pinot

AATD has come to the conclusion that it's going to need to introduce a new piece of infrastructure to achieve scalable real-time analytics, but isn't yet convinced that a full-blown OLAP database is necessary.

In this chapter, we'll start by explaining why we can't just use a stream processor to serve queries on streams, before introducing Apache Pinot, one of the new breed of OLAP databases designed for real-time analytics. We'll learn about Pinot's architecture and data model, before ingesting the orders stream. After that, we'll learn about timestamp indexes and how to write queries against Pinot using SQL.

Figure 5-1 shows how we're going to evolve our infrastructure in this chapter.

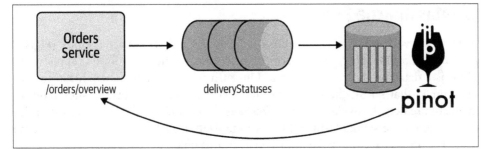

Figure 5-1. Evolution of the orders service

Why Can't We Use Another Stream Processor?

At the end of the last chapter, we described some of the limitations of using Kafka Streams to serve queries on top of streams. (See "Limitations of Kafka Streams" on page 60.) These were by no means a criticism of Kafka Streams as a technology; it's just that we weren't really using it for the types of problems for which it was designed.

A reasonable question might be, Why can't we use another stream processor instead, such as ksqlDB or Flink? Both of these tools offer SQL interfaces, solving the issue of having to write Java code to query streams.

Unfortunately, it still doesn't get us past the underlying problem: stream processing tools aren't built for running analytics queries at scale. These tools excel when we're building stream processing applications and are perfect for filtering streams, joining streams, creating alerts, and so on.

We could certainly build a real-time analytics application for internal use with one of these tools, and it would likely scale perfectly well for this type of usage. However, if we want to build something that scales to tens or thousands of requests per second, we'll need to introduce an OLAP database that's custom built for this situation.

Why Can't We Use a Data Warehouse?

Data warehouses are a form of OLAP database, but they aren't suitable for real-time analytics because they don't satisfy the requirements that we identified in Chapter 2, which were ingestion latency, query latency, and concurrency.

Batch ETL pipelines are commonly used to populate big data warehouses such as Big-Query or Redshift. However, this causes ingestion latency and makes the data outdated when queried. Moreover, their query engines are not optimized for millisecond latency, but for ad hoc querying with acceptable latencies in the seconds. Finally, our serving layer needs to scale to thousands of queries per second if we're building user-facing applications, which isn't the sweet spot of data warehouses.

What Is Apache Pinot?

Instead we will use a real-time OLAP database, and it's Apache Pinot (*https://pinot.apache.org*) that is going to perform the role of serving layer for our application. Pinot is a database that was created at LinkedIn in 2013, after the engineering staff determined that no off-the-shelf solutions met the social networking site's requirements of predictable low latency, data freshness in seconds, fault tolerance, and scalability. These are essential features for any organization that wants to obtain real-time insights from its data and make informed decisions quickly.

Pinot was donated to the Apache Software Foundation in June 2019, where it has continued to evolve and improve. An architecture diagram of Apache Pinot is in Figure 5-2.

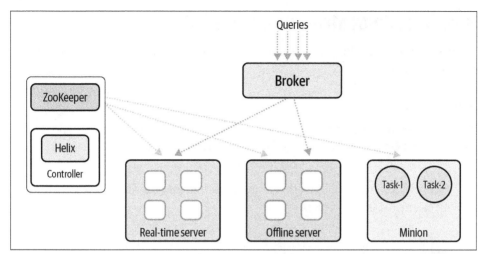

Figure 5-2. Apache Pinot architecture

We will initially be using Pinot to consume events from the orders topic and then provide a way for us to query those events.

Pinot's components and a description of their responsibilities are as follows:

Controller
Maintains global metadata, manages other Pinot components, provides admin endpoints, provides endpoints for segment upload, and takes care of other management activities.

Broker
Receives queries from clients and forwards them to the right servers, before collecting the results and consolidating them into a single response to send back to the client.

Server
Hosts data segments and serves queries off the hosted data. Offline and real-time servers are shown as separate components, but are both responsible for serving data. Offline means that data has been ingested using a batch process; real-time means it was ingested from a streaming data platform.

Minion
An optional component that's used to execute computationally intensive tasks that would otherwise be done by other components.

How Does Pinot Model and Store Data?

Pinot stores data in tables that have corresponding schemas. Let's go through those concepts in turn.

Schema

The schema defines the fields in a Pinot table, along with their data types and default values. Each field fits into one of the following categories:

Dimension
Used in slice-and-dice operations for answering queries. These fields are used in WHERE and GROUP BY clauses.

 Slice and dice describes the process of breaking large datasets into smaller ones for visualization and further analysis. It involves selecting, filtering, and aggregating data based on different attributes like location or product/customer demographics.

Metric
Used to represent quantitative data. These columns are used for aggregation by means of the SUM, MIN, MAX, COUNT, and AVG functions, but they can also be used in WHERE clauses.

DateTime
Used to represent time columns. There can be multiple time columns, but one must be specified as the primary time column, which maintains the time boundary between offline and real-time data in a hybrid table. These columns are used in GROUP BY and WHERE clauses.

When creating a schema, we need to keep the data source in mind so that we map our fields correctly. Pinot will automatically map columns that have the same name as the property keys in the data source. For example, if we have an event with the key id and a column with the name id, the data for this column will be automatically mapped.

Table

A *table* in Pinot is a logical abstraction that represents a collection of related data. It is composed of columns and rows or documents.

A table can be one of the following types:

Offline
Offline tables ingest prebuilt Pinot segments from external data stores. Used for batch ingestion.

Real-time
> Real-time tables ingest data from streams (such as Kafka) and build segments from the consumed data.

Hybrid
> A hybrid Pinot table is comprised of both real-time and offline tables that have the same name.

Within a table, data is stored in segments, which contain the data for all the columns, but a subset of rows. These segments can be distributed across servers and will be replicated on multiple servers in a typical production setup.

Setup

We're going to build upon the Docker Compose configuration that we defined in the preceding chapter. You can find the full Docker Compose file (*https://oreil.ly/qxuMp*) used in this chapter in the book's GitHub repository.

Let's go through the extra components that we've added from the Docker Compose file that we saw in "Setup" on page 37.

Pinot is an OLAP database that will perform the role of serving layer in this application. The Docker Compose config for a Pinot controller, broker, and server is defined in Example 5-1.

Example 5-1. docker-compose-pinot.yml

```
pinot-controller:
  image: apachepinot/pinot:0.10.0
  command: "StartController -zkAddress zookeeper:2181"
  container_name: "pinot-controller"
  restart: unless-stopped
  ports:
    - "9000:9000"
  depends_on:
    - zookeeper
pinot-broker:
  image: apachepinot/pinot:0.10.0
  command: "StartBroker -zkAddress zookeeper:2181"
  restart: unless-stopped
  container_name: "pinot-broker"
  ports:
    - "8099:8099"
  depends_on:
    - pinot-controller
pinot-server:
  image: apachepinot/pinot:0.10.0
  container_name: "pinot-server"
  command: "StartServer -zkAddress zookeeper:2181"
```

```
  restart: unless-stopped
  depends_on:
    - pinot-broker
```

We can spin up all the containers by running the following command:

```
docker-compose \
  -f docker-compose-base.yml \
  -f docker-compose-pinot.yml \
  up
```

Once that's up and running, we're ready to start loading data into Pinot.

Data Ingestion

To recap, one of the messages from the `orders` stream is shown in Example 5-2.

Example 5-2. A message from the `orders` stream

```
{
  "id": "3d0d442f-1afc-494a-8c75-0e67fa8b31d4",
  "createdAt": "2022-09-06T10:46:17.481843",
  "userId": 521,
  "status": "PLACED_ORDER",
  "price": 5626,
  "items": [
    {"productId": "43", "quantity": 2, "price": 609},
    {"productId": "20", "quantity": 3, "price": 85},
    {"productId": "14", "quantity": 2, "price": 569},
    {"productId": "75", "quantity": 4, "price": 255},
    {"productId": "24", "quantity": 4, "price": 215},
    {"productId": "36", "quantity": 5, "price": 60},
    {"productId": "75", "quantity": 1, "price": 255},
    {"productId": "25", "quantity": 4, "price": 145}
  ]
}
```

We will use `createdAt` as our DateTime field, `price` will be a metric field, and all the others will be dimensions. The schema that we're going to use is shown in Example 5-3.

Example 5-3. pinot/config/orders/schema.json

```
{
  "schemaName": "orders",
  "dimensionFieldSpecs": [
    {"name": "id", "dataType": "STRING"},
    {"name": "userId", "dataType": "INT"},
    {"name": "status", "dataType": "STRING"},
    {"name": "items", "dataType": "JSON"}
  ],
```

```
  "metricFieldSpecs": [
    {"name": "productsOrdered", "dataType": "INT"},
    {"name": "totalQuantity", "dataType": "INT"},
    {"name": "price", "dataType": "DOUBLE"}
  ],
  "dateTimeFieldSpecs": [
    {
      "name": "ts",
      "dataType": "TIMESTAMP",
      "format": "1:MILLISECONDS:EPOCH",
      "granularity": "1:MILLISECONDS"
    }
  ]
}
```

One of the interesting things in this schema is that the data type of the items column is JSON. Pinot doesn't currently have a map data type, so JSON is the best choice for this type of data.

We can create the schema by running the following command:

```
docker run -v $PWD/pinot/config:/config \
  --network rta \
  apachepinot/pinot:0.10.0 \
  AddSchema -schemaFile /config/orders/schema.json \
  -controllerHost pinot-controller \
  -exec
```

The table config is shown in Example 5-4.

Example 5-4. pinot/config/orders/table.json

```
{
  "tableName": "orders",
  "tableType": "REALTIME", ❶
  "segmentsConfig": {
    "schemaName": "orders", ❷
    "timeColumnName": "ts", ❸
    "timeType": "MILLISECONDS",
    "replicasPerPartition": "1"
  },
  "tenants": {},
  "tableIndexConfig": {
    "loadMode": "MMAP",
    "streamConfigs": {
      "streamType": "kafka",
      "stream.kafka.consumer.type": "lowLevel", ❹
      "stream.kafka.topic.name": "orders",
      "stream.kafka.decoder.class.name":
        "org.apache.pinot.plugin.stream.kafka.KafkaJSONMessageDecoder",
      "stream.kafka.consumer.factory.class.name":
        "org.apache.pinot.plugin.stream.kafka20.KafkaConsumerFactory",
```

```
    "stream.kafka.broker.list": "kafka:9092",
    "stream.kafka.consumer.prop.auto.offset.reset": "smallest"  ❺
  }
},
"ingestionConfig": {
  "transformConfigs": [  ❻
    {
      "columnName": "ts",
      "transformFunction":
          "FromDateTime(createdAt, 'yyyy-MM-dd''T''HH:mm:ss.SSSSSS')"  ❼
    }
  ]
},
"metadata": {"customConfigs": {}},
"routing": {"instanceSelectorType": "strictReplicaGroup"}
}
```

❶ REALTIME table because we're ingesting streaming data.

❷ Name of the schema associated with this table.

❸ Name of the primary DateTime column specified in the schema.

❹ lowLevel means Pinot will process data from Kafka topic partitions in parallel. The alternative is highlevel, which would treat incoming data as one big partition.

❺ Ingests data from Kafka topic partitions starting from the earliest available offset.

❻ Functions that transform the source data before it is pushed into Pinot.

❼ Converts the createdAt DateTime string to epoch milliseconds.

At the moment, this table doesn't have any explicit indexes configured, but we can add those indexes at a later point.

We can create the table by running the following command:

```
docker run -v $PWD/pinot/config:/config \
  --network rta \
  apachepinot/pinot:0.10.0 \
  AddTable -tableConfigFile /config/orders/table.json \
  -controllerHost pinot-controller \
  -exec
```

Once the table and schema have been created, Pinot will automatically start ingesting the data that has already been ingested into Kafka. It will also ingest any future data published into the orders topic.

Pinot Data Explorer

If we navigate to *localhost:9000*, we'll see the Pinot Data Explorer (*https://oreil.ly/rRcEt*), which we can use to query the orders table. Let's click the Query Console icon and then run this query:

```
select userId, count(*)
from orders
group by userId
order by count(*) DESC
```

The results of running this query can be seen in Table 5-1.

Table 5-1. Number of orders by userId

userId	count(*)
696	221
448	220
212	219
356	217
637	216
82	214
610	214
133	213
305	212
225	211

Another thing we might want to know is how many orders have been made recently. We can work out the number of orders each minute by running the following query:

```
SELECT dateTrunc('MINUTE', ts) AS minute, count(*)
FROM orders
GROUP BY minute
ORDER BY minute DESC
LIMIT 5
```

The results of running this query can be seen in Table 5-2.

Table 5-2. Number of orders made per minute

minute	count(*)
1661348760000	752
1661348700000	997
1661348640000	993
1661348580000	991
1661348520000	997

To reproduce the results that we got with our Kafka Streams at the end of the previous chapter, we'll need to count the number of events and total revenue in the last minute and the previous minute. We can do that with the following query:

```
select count(*) FILTER(WHERE  ts > ago('PT1M')) AS events1Min,
       count(*) FILTER(WHERE  ts <= ago('PT1M') AND ts > ago('PT2M'))
           AS events1Min2Min,
       sum("price") FILTER(WHERE  ts > ago('PT1M')) AS total1Min,
       sum("price") FILTER(WHERE  ts <= ago('PT1M') AND ts > ago('PT2M'))
           AS total1Min2Min
from orders
where ts > ago('PT2M')
limit 1
```

The results of running this query can be seen in Table 5-3.

Table 5-3. Recent orders and revenue

events1Min	events1Min2Min	total1Min	total1Min2Min
999	984	4375430	4240416

Indexes

Apache Pinot supports lots of indexes, including inverted, JSON, range, geospatial, timestamp, and text. These indexes are defined via the table config and are applied on a segment-by-segment basis. This means that one segment in a table could have an index defined on a column, while another segment in that same table doesn't.

Indexes can be defined at the time of table creation or afterward. If we define them afterward we'll need to re-create existing segments because the implementation of indexes is contained within segment files.

We can make queries that filter or aggregate on timestamp fields quicker by applying a timestamp index. Timestamp indexes can be applied to only columns with the TIME STAMP type. When we apply this index, a new column will be added for each granularity and those columns will have a range index. In addition, any queries that use the dateTrunc function will be rewritten to use the new column instead.

To add a timestamp index, we need to specify the following:

- Encoding type (default is DICTIONARY)
- Index types (a one-element array with the value TIMESTAMP)
- Granularities for the index

These properties are all configured under the top-level fieldConfigList key, as shown in this partial table config:

```
{
  ...
  "fieldConfigList": [
    {
      "name": "ts",
      "encodingType": "DICTIONARY",
      "indexTypes": ["TIMESTAMP"],
      "timestampConfig": {"granularities": ["MINUTE","HOUR"]}
    }
  ],
  ...
}
```

With this configuration, Pinot will create an extra column for each granularity—for example, tsMINUTE and tsHOUR. It will assign these values to the columns:

- tsMINUTE = dateTrunc('MINUTE', ts)

- tsHOUR = dateTrunc('HOUR', ts)

Pinot will also add a range index for the new fields, as well as rewrite any queries that use the dateTrunc function with MINUTE or HOUR and the ts field. Therefore, this query:

```
SELECT dateTrunc('MINUTE', ts) AS minute, count(*)
FROM wikievents
GROUP BY minute
ORDER BY minute DESC
LIMIT 5
```

gets rewritten to this:

```
SELECT $ts$MINUTE AS minute, count(*)
FROM wikievents
GROUP BY minute
ORDER BY minute DESC
LIMIT 5
```

We can update the table config by using the HTTP API:

```
curl -X PUT "http://localhost:9000/tables/orders" \
  -H "accept: application/json" \
  -H "Content-Type: application/json" \
  -d @config/table_with-index.json
```

New segments will automatically pick up the timestamp index, but you'll need to call the endpoint that reloads existing segments to add the timestamp index to existing segments:

```
curl -X POST "http://localhost:9000/segments/orders/reload?forceDownload=false" \
  -H "accept: application/json"
```

We can now rerun the previous queries and should see the same results, but we probably won't see a discernible speed-up until the data volume increases.

Updating the Web App

Finally, we need to update the web application that we started building in the previous chapter to add an endpoint that returns an overview of orders based on data stored in Pinot. (See "Quarkus Application" on page 53.) We'll need to update the *pom.xml* file to include the Pinot Java client and jOOQ SQL query generator:

```
<dependency>
    <groupId>org.apache.pinot</groupId>
    <artifactId>pinot-java-client</artifactId>
    <version>0.11.0</version>
</dependency>

<dependency>
    <groupId>org.jooq</groupId>
    <artifactId>jooq</artifactId>
    <version>3.17.4</version>
</dependency>
```

We'll add a new method to OrdersResource, so that this class now looks like this:

```
package pizzashop.rest;

import org.apache.pinot.client.Connection;
import org.apache.pinot.client.ConnectionFactory;
import org.apache.pinot.client.ResultSet;
import org.apache.pinot.client.ResultSetGroup;
import org.jooq.SQLDialect;
import org.jooq.impl.DSL;
import pizzashop.models.OrdersSummary;
import pizzashop.models.PinotOrdersSummary;
import pizzashop.models.TimePeriod;
import pizzashop.streams.InteractiveQueries;

import javax.enterprise.context.ApplicationScoped;
import javax.inject.Inject;
import javax.ws.rs.GET;
import javax.ws.rs.Path;
import javax.ws.rs.core.Response;

import static org.jooq.impl.DSL.*;

@ApplicationScoped
@Path("/orders")
public class OrdersResource {
    @Inject
    InteractiveQueries interactiveQueries;
```

```
private Connection connection = ConnectionFactory.fromHostList(
    "localhost:8099");

@GET
@Path("/overview")
public Response overview() {
    OrdersSummary ordersSummary = interactiveQueries.ordersSummary();
    return Response.ok(ordersSummary).build();
}

@GET
@Path("/overview2")
public Response overview2() {
    ResultSet resultSet = runQuery(connection,
        "select count(*) from orders limit 10");
    int totalOrders = resultSet.getInt(0);

    String query = DSL.using(SQLDialect.POSTGRES).select(
            count()
                .filterWhere("ts > ago('PT1M')")
                .as("events1Min"),

            count()
                .filterWhere("ts <= ago('PT1M') AND ts > ago('PT2M')")
                .as("events1Min2Min"),

            sum(field("price").coerce(Long.class))
                .filterWhere("ts > ago('PT1M')")
                .as("total1Min"),

            sum(field("price").coerce(Long.class))
                .filterWhere("ts <= ago('PT1M') AND ts > ago('PT2M')")
                .as("total1Min2Min")

    ).from("orders").getSQL();

    ResultSet summaryResults = runQuery(connection, query);

    TimePeriod currentTimePeriod = new TimePeriod(
            summaryResults.getLong(0, 0), summaryResults.getDouble(0, 2));
    TimePeriod previousTimePeriod = new TimePeriod(
            summaryResults.getLong(0, 1), summaryResults.getDouble(0, 3));
    PinotOrdersSummary ordersSummary = new PinotOrdersSummary(
            totalOrders, currentTimePeriod, previousTimePeriod);

    return Response.ok(ordersSummary).build();
}

private static ResultSet runQuery(Connection connection, String query) {
    ResultSetGroup resultSetGroup = connection.execute(query);
    return resultSetGroup.getResultSet(0);
```

```
      }
    }
```

We've added a new endpoint, /orders/overview2, in which we create a connection to a Pinot broker and then execute a couple of queries, which do the following:

- Get the total count of number of orders
- Compute the number of orders in the last minute, the number of orders in the minute before that, the revenue generated in the last minute, and the revenue generated in the minute before that

We then create a `PinotOrdersSummary` instance that contains all this information. `PinotOrdersSummary` has the same fields as `OrdersSummary`, so we won't include the code for that class here, but you can find it in the book's GitHub repository.

Once we've done that, our Quarkus app should have automatically refreshed, and we can query the new endpoint:

```
curl http://localhost:8080/orders/overview2 2>/dev/null | jq '.'
```

We should see the output in Example 5-5.

Example 5-5. Latest orders state

```
{
  "totalOrders": 183798,
  "currentTimePeriod": {
    "orders": 986,
    "totalPrice": 4290349
  },
  "previousTimePeriod": {
    "orders": 1008,
    "totalPrice": 4476211
  }
}
```

Summary

In this chapter, we learned how to set up Apache Pinot as the serving layer in our real-time analytics architecture. We created a schema and table and added a time-stamp index, before adding a new endpoint to the Quarkus app that returns the results from querying Pinot.

While JSON is a perfectly fine format for consumption by the engineering team, our operations team would like a UI on top of this data, and that's exactly what we're going to do in the next chapter.

CHAPTER 6

Building a Real-Time Analytics Dashboard

In this chapter, we're going to learn how to build a real-time analytics dashboard for AATD's operators. This dashboard will be built on top of the orders service that we introduced in Chapter 4 and then extended in Chapter 5.

We'll stream the data from Kafka into Pinot and build a Streamlit dashboard that gives an overview of revenue and total orders over time. The application that we build in this chapter will fit into the internal/human-facing quadrant that was introduced in "Classifying Real-Time Analytics Applications" on page 9, as shown in Figure 6-1.

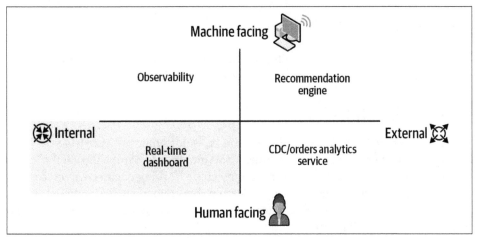

Figure 6-1. Real-time analytics quadrant: human/internal

Dashboard Architecture

For the first version of our dashboard, we're going to be building on top of the orders service introduced in Chapter 3 (see Figure 3-3). Apache Pinot will consume events from the orders topic, and we'll then query Pinot from our Streamlit dashboard. Figure 6-2 gives an overview of the system that we're going to build.

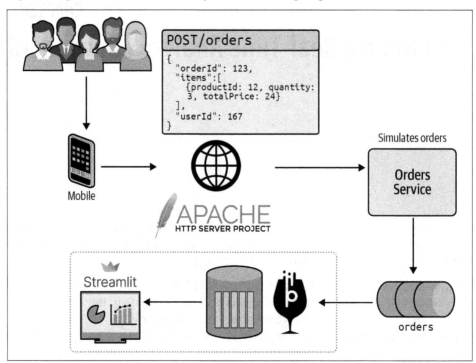

Figure 6-2. Dashboard v1 architecture diagram

The new components in the architecture are included inside the dotted box. Next, we're going to update our Docker infrastructure to add these new components.

What Is Streamlit?

Streamlit (*https://streamlit.io*) is an open source web framework that lets you build web applications using only Python code. It was developed with the goal of making it easy for data scientists, data engineers, and machine learning engineers to create and share data applications without having to learn web technologies. Streamlit provides a simple and intuitive API and integrates with popular Python data libraries including pandas, Plotly, and scikit-learn.

Setup

We're going to build upon the Docker Compose configuration files that we used in the previous chapters. You can find these files in the book's GitHub repository. The Docker compose config for our Streamlit dashboard is shown in Example 6-1.

Example 6-1. docker-compose-dashboard.yaml

```yaml
dashboard:
    build: streamlit
    restart: unless-stopped
    container_name: dashboard
    ports:
      - "8501:8501"
    depends_on:
      - pinot-controller
    volumes:
      - ./streamlit/app.py:/workdir/app.py
    environment:
      - PINOT_SERVER
      - PINOT_PORT
```

The `streamlit` directory contains an `app.py` file with the complete code built in this chapter, but let's have a look at how we'd go about building it from scratch.

Building the Dashboard

Let's start building our dashboard. We're going to be using Python to do this, so let's first create a virtual environment:

```
python -m venv .venv
source .venv/bin/activate
```

 We are using the built-in virtual environment feature, but feel free to use your preferred choice—or not, as the case may be!

Now, we need to install Streamlit by running the following command:

```
pip install streamlit
```

Create a file called *app.py*, and add the following code to import libraries and configure the page:

```
import streamlit as st
import requests

st.set_page_config(layout="wide")
st.header("Pizza App Dashboard")

delivery_service_api = "http://kafka-streams-quarkus:8080"
```

Now call the `overview` endpoint that we created in the previous chapter:

```
response = requests.get(f"{delivery_service_api}/orders/overview2").json()
st.write(response)
```

We can run the application using Streamlit with the following command:

```
streamlit run app.py
```

Navigate to *localhost:8501*, and you should see the information in Figure 6-3.

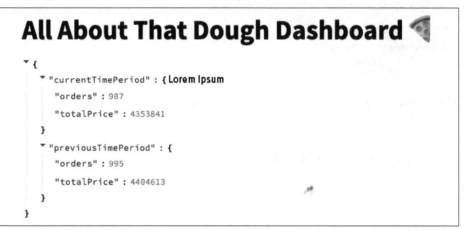

Figure 6-3. Recent orders JSON

So far, so good, but we can improve the data display.

Streamlit includes the concept of a metric, which takes in a value and a delta. Let's create metrics for the number of orders, revenue generated, and average revenue per order:

```
current = response["currentTimePeriod"]
prev = response["previousTimePeriod"]

metric1, metric2, metric3 = st.columns(3)

metric1.metric(
    label="# of Orders",
    value="{:,}".format(current["orders"]),
    delta="{:,}".format(int(current["orders"] - prev["orders"])))
)

metric2.metric(
    label="Revenue in",
    value="{:,}".format(current["totalPrice"]),
    delta="{:,}".format(int(current["totalPrice"] - prev["totalPrice"])))
)

ave_order_value_1min = current["totalPrice"] / int(current["orders"])
```

```
ave_order_value_1min_2min = (prev["totalPrice"] / int(prev["orders"]))

metric3.metric(
    label="Average order value",
    value="{:,.2f}".format(ave_order_value_1min),
    delta="{:,.2f}".format(ave_order_value_1min - ave_order_value_1min_2min)
)
```

The Streamlit dashboard will be automatically updated with these changes, so let's go back to the web browser to see. We can see the new dashboard in Figure 6-4.

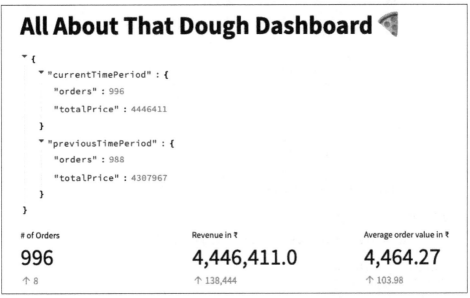

All About That Dough Dashboard

```
▾ {
    ▾ "currentTimePeriod" : {
        "orders" : 996
        "totalPrice" : 4446411
    }
    ▾ "previousTimePeriod" : {
        "orders" : 988
        "totalPrice" : 4307967
    }
}
```

# of Orders	Revenue in ₹	Average order value in ₹
996	**4,446,411.0**	**4,464.27**
↑ 8	↑ 138,444	↑ 103.98

Figure 6-4. Recent orders metrics

We can now remove the JSON rendering, since that's been superseded by the metrics.

The metrics show the changes in the last couple of minutes, but we'd quite like to see what's going on over a longer period of time. To do this, we'll need to update our Quarkus application to return the number of orders and revenue bucketed by minute. Add a new endpoint to OrdersSource, /orders/ordersPerMinute, defined here:

```
@GET
@Path("/ordersPerMinute")
public Response ordersPerMinute() {
    String query = DSL.using(SQLDialect.POSTGRES)
            .select(
                    field("ToDateTime(DATETRUNC('MINUTE', ts),
                      'yyyy-MM-dd HH:mm:ss')")
                        .as("dateMin"),
                    count(field("*")),
                    sum(field("price").coerce(Long.class))
```

```
                )
                .from("orders")
                .groupBy(field("dateMin"))
                .orderBy(field("dateMin").desc())
                .$where(field("dateMin").greaterThan(field("ago('PT1H')")))
                .$limit(DSL.inline(60))
                .getSQL();

        ResultSet summaryResults = runQuery(connection, query);

        int rowCount = summaryResults.getRowCount();

        List<SummaryRow> rows = new ArrayList<>();
        for (int index = 0; index < rowCount; index++) {
            rows.add(new SummaryRow(
                    summaryResults.getString(index, 0),
                    summaryResults.getLong(index, 1),
                    summaryResults.getDouble(index, 2)
            ));
        }

        return Response.ok(rows).build();
    }
```

SummaryRow.java is defined as follows:

```
package pizzashop.models;

import io.quarkus.runtime.annotations.RegisterForReflection;

@RegisterForReflection
public class SummaryRow {
    private final String timestamp;
    private final long orders;
    private final double revenue;

    public SummaryRow(String timestamp, long orders, double revenue) {
        this.timestamp = timestamp;
        this.orders = orders;
        this.revenue = revenue;
    }

    public String getTimestamp() {return timestamp;}
    public long getOrders() {return orders;}
    public double getRevenue() {return revenue;}
}
```

This endpoint returns a list of orders/revenue grouped by minute:

```
curl http://localhost:8080/orders/ordersPerMinute 2>/dev/null | jq -c '.[]'
```

The output of running this command is shown in Example 6-2.

Example 6-2. Latest orders state

```
{"timestamp":"2022-11-21 15:26:00","orders":598,"revenue":2589579}
{"timestamp":"2022-11-21 15:25:00","orders":996,"revenue":4489957}
{"timestamp":"2022-11-21 15:24:00","orders":992,"revenue":4404577}
{"timestamp":"2022-11-21 15:23:00","orders":969,"revenue":4235964}
{"timestamp":"2022-11-21 15:22:00","orders":1010,"revenue":4510812}
{"timestamp":"2022-11-21 15:21:00","orders":986,"revenue":4321972}
{"timestamp":"2022-11-21 15:20:00","orders":990,"revenue":4329701}
{"timestamp":"2022-11-21 15:19:00","orders":990,"revenue":4507306}
{"timestamp":"2022-11-21 15:18:00","orders":994,"revenue":4366150}
{"timestamp":"2022-11-21 15:17:00","orders":978,"revenue":4225961}
{"timestamp":"2022-11-21 15:16:00","orders":983,"revenue":4187605}
{"timestamp":"2022-11-21 15:15:00","orders":973,"revenue":4200897}
{"timestamp":"2022-11-21 15:14:00","orders":996,"revenue":4423180}
{"timestamp":"2022-11-21 15:13:00","orders":980,"revenue":4296573}
{"timestamp":"2022-11-21 15:12:00","orders":975,"revenue":4308728}
{"timestamp":"2022-11-21 15:11:00","orders":637,"revenue":2878460}
```

Now let's go back to our dashboard app and have it use this new endpoint.

We're going to create a line chart of these values by using the Plotly charting library, so let's first install that:

```
pip install plotly
```

We'll need to update the imports section of our script to include Plotly as well as pandas, since we'll be using both of these tools in the next section:

```
import pandas as pd
import plotly.graph_objects as go
```

We can then add the following code to call the API endpoint and put the results into a DataFrame:

```
response = requests.get(f"{delivery_service_api}/orders/ordersPerMinute").json()
df_ts = pd.DataFrame(response)
```

We'll then reshape the DataFrame to the format expected by Plotly by using the `pd.melt` function:

```
df_ts_melt = pd.melt(
    frame=df_ts,
    id_vars=['timestamp'],
    value_vars=['orders', 'revenue']
)
```

A subset of the values in the melted DataFrame can be seen in Table 6-1.

Table 6-1. Revenue and orders at 03:36 on August 24, 2022

dateMin	variable	value
2022-08-24 03:36:00	revenue	757,744.0000

dateMin	variable	value
2022-08-24 03:36:00	orders	979.0000

Finally, we can render the DataFrame as a couple of line charts:

```python
# Split the canvas into two vertical columns
col1, col2 = st.columns(2)
with col1:
    orders = df_ts_melt[df_ts_melt.variable == "orders"]

    fig = go.FigureWidget(data=[
        go.Scatter(x=orders.timestamp,
                   y=orders.value, mode='lines',
                   line={'dash': 'solid', 'color': 'green'})
    ])
    fig.update_layout(showlegend=False, title="Orders per minute",
                      margin=dict(l=0, r=0, t=40, b=0),)
    fig.update_yaxes(range=[0, df_ts["orders"].max() * 1.1])
    st.plotly_chart(fig, use_container_width=True)

with col2:
    revenue = df_ts_melt[df_ts_melt.variable == "revenue"]

    fig = go.FigureWidget(data=[
        go.Scatter(x=revenue.timestamp,
                   y=revenue.value, mode='lines',
                   line={'dash': 'solid', 'color': 'blue'})
    ])
    fig.update_layout(showlegend=False, title="Revenue per minute",
                      margin=dict(l=0, r=0, t=40, b=0),)
    fig.update_yaxes(range=[0, df_ts["revenue"].max() * 1.1])
    st.plotly_chart(fig, use_container_width=True)
```

The result of adding these charts can be seen in Figure 6-5.

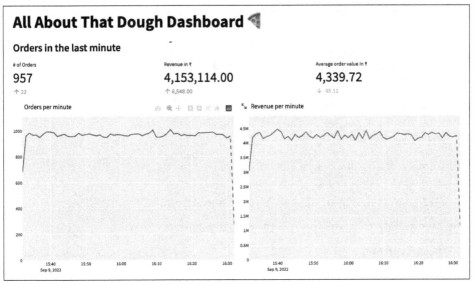

Figure 6-5. Recent orders line chart

At the moment, we have to manually refresh the web browser to see the latest changes, which isn't an ideal user experience. We can make the dashboard auto refreshing using the `st.experimental_rerun` function.

We're going to introduce two bits of state:

`auto_refresh`
    Whether the dashboard should automatically refresh

`sleep_time`
    How often it should refresh (in seconds)

First, let's import some libraries:

```
import time
from datetime import datetime
```

And now we'll add the following code just below `st.header`:

```
now = datetime.now()
dt_string = now.strftime("%d %B %Y %H:%M:%S")
st.write(f"Last update: {dt_string}")

if not "sleep_time" in st.session_state:
    st.session_state.sleep_time = 2 ❶

if not "auto_refresh" in st.session_state:
    st.session_state.auto_refresh = True ❷
```

```
auto_refresh = st.checkbox('Auto Refresh?', st.session_state.auto_refresh)

if auto_refresh:
    number = st.number_input('Refresh rate in seconds',
      value=st.session_state.sleep_time) ❸
    st.session_state.sleep_time = number

# The rest of the dashboard code goes here
```

❶ `sleep_time` defaults to 2 seconds.

❷ `auto_refresh` defaults to `True`.

❸ Set `sleep_time` if the dashboard should auto refresh.

And then add the following code to the end of the file:

```
if auto_refresh:
    time.sleep(number)
    st.experimental_rerun() ❶
```

❶ `st.experimental_rerun` (*https://oreil.ly/6uohs*) is a function that forces the whole script to be rerun from the top immediately. At the time of writing, this is the best way to achieve auto refresh functionality.

If we go back to our web browser, we'll see something like Figure 6-6.

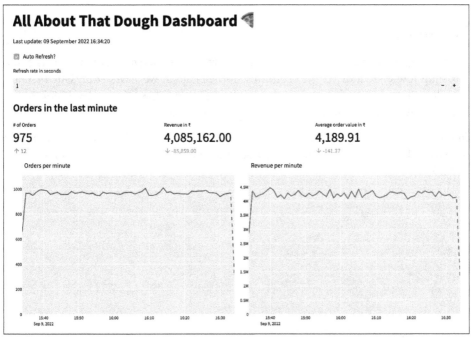

Figure 6-6. Auto refreshing dashboard

The dashboard is now automatically refreshing on the interval that we specify, which is exactly what we wanted. So far, our dashboard contains data showing revenue and the number of orders over time, but we don't have anything about products, which is one of our requirements.

The orders stream doesn't currently contain anything beyond the ID of the products that have been ordered, but in the next chapter we'll learn how to enrich orders with product information and then update the dashboard accordingly.

Summary

In this chapter, we've learned how to build a real-time analytics dashboard with the Streamlit low-code tool. At the beginning of the chapter, we started out with a stream of orders in Apache Kafka, and, in the pages that followed, we connected Pinot to that stream of events and built visualizations on top of the data.

In the next chapter, we'll learn about change data capture, a technique that we can use to extract data from our MySQL database and combine it with the data that we have in Kafka.

CHAPTER 7

Product Changes Captured with Change Data Capture

The operations team at AATD is now able to get a solid overview of the number of orders and the revenue that the business is making. What's missing is that they don't know what's happening at the product level. Complaints from other parts of the business indicate that some products are seeing surges in orders while there's too much stock for other items.

The data about individual products is currently stored in the MySQL database, but we need to get it out of there and into our real-time analytics architecture. In this chapter, we'll learn how to do this using a technique called *change data capture* (CDC).

Capturing Changes from Operational Databases

Businesses often record their transactions in operational, or OLTP, databases. Businesses often want to analyze their operational data, but how should they go about doing that?

Traditionally, ETL pipelines have been used to move data from operational databases to analytical databases like data warehouses. Those pipelines were executed periodically, extracting data from source databases in large batches. After that, the data was transformed before loading it into the analytics database.

The problem with this classic approach was the significant latency between data collection and decision making. For example, a typical batch pipeline would take minutes, hours, or days to generate insights from operational data.

What if there was a mechanism to capture changes made to source databases in real time as they happen? This is where CDC technology comes into the scene.

Change Data Capture

In this section, we'll define CDC and explain why we need it, before describing techniques for achieving it. We'll conclude by describing Debezium, which has emerged as the de facto standard of CDC tools.

Why Do We Need CDC?

When we start building an application, we can often get away with using a single database for all our data needs. But as our application evolves, we'll start to have different data access patterns and require different data models.

This may lead us to explore using multiple data tools to handle the various problems that we encounter. For example, we may need a search engine to perform full-text searches, a cache to speed up reads, or a data warehouse to perform complex historical analytics on data.

Figure 7-1 shows how an application might use multiple data systems.

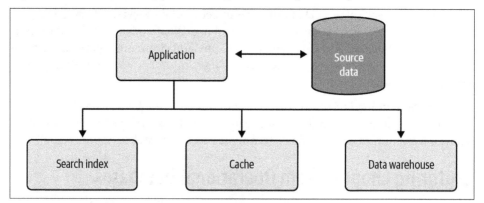

Figure 7-1. An application with data in multiple places

Having data in multiple systems introduces some new problems regarding the *source of truth* of the data. The source of truth of a piece of data is the authoritative version. If there are discrepancies between the data from different systems, we will trust the source of truth.

So we need to specify one of our data sources as the source of truth. Other systems can then take that source data, apply their own transformations to it, and store it in their own representations, as illustrated in Figure 7-2. These systems are effectively operating on derived data; if they lose the data, it doesn't really matter because it can be re-created from the source of truth.

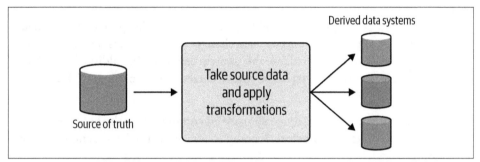

Figure 7-2. Source of truth and derived data systems

Source data and derived data need to stay in sync to preserve consistency across our applications. If there's an update in the source data, it must be reflected in the derived data. If a record is deleted from the source, that record should also be deleted from downstream systems.

There needs to be a way of capturing the changes from the source of truth and reliably propagating them to derived data systems. Enter change data capture!

What Is CDC?

Change data capture (*https://oreil.ly/Tra5J*) describes the process of capturing the changes made to data in a source system and then making them available to downstream/derived data systems. These changes could be new records, changes to existing records, or deleted records.

Although the term CDC is relatively new, the underlying concept has been present in the industry as *database replication* and *extract, transform, load* (ETL). These approaches tend to be complex, require expensive licensing, and are too slow. Hence, organizations were on the lookout for a real-time, event-driven way to synchronize source and target data systems.

What Are the Strategies for Implementing CDC?

There are several strategies for implementing CDC. These are some of the most popular techniques:

Polling
> This involves polling the LAST_UPDATED column of tables periodically to detect changes. This approach doesn't capture changes in real time, is unable to identify deleted rows, and puts load on the source database. In addition, if a LAST_ UPDATED column doesn't exist in the source database, it would need to be added.

Snapshots
> Another technique is to take snapshots. We'd compute the delta between the current and previous deltas before sending it downstream. This technique would capture deletes.

Triggers
> Database triggers can be used to capture row-level changes. This approach captures changes in real time, but it's resource intensive and can slow down other workloads on the source database.

Log-based data capture
> Relational databases have long had change logs that describe all the operations applied to the database. We can watch these logs with minimal performance impact. This technique is naturally streaming; change logs capture transactions that contain changes in a table, and those are events. Many CDC systems use this as their underlying technique.

Log-Based Data Capture

Let's go into log-based data capture, or *transaction log tailing* as it's sometimes known, in a bit more detail to understand how it works.

Users and applications make changes to the source database in the form of inserts, updates, and deletes. These changes are captured in the transaction log before they're applied to the data store.

The CDC system watches the transaction log for any changes and propagates them into the target system, while preserving the change order. The target system then replays the changes to update its internal state. Figure 7-3 shows how this works.

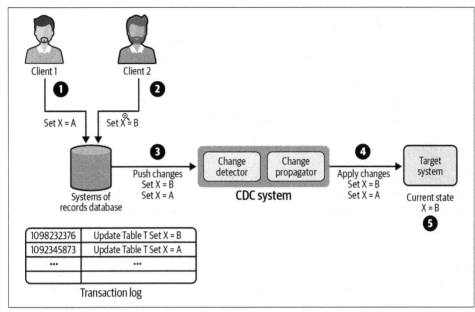

Figure 7-3. Theoretical view of a CDC system

In Figure 7-3, Client 1 and Client 2 update the value of X in two transactions. The transaction log records the changes. Eventually, the CDC system picks up the changes and delivers them to the destination so that the changes can be replayed to target systems.

That looks straightforward in theory, but designing a production-grade CDC system requires prior planning in terms of scalability, reliability, and extensibility.

Requirements for a CDC System

A production-grade CDC system should satisfy the following needs:

Message ordering guarantee
The order of changes *must be* preserved so that they are propagated to the target systems as is.

Pub/sub
Should support asynchronous, pub/sub-style change propagation to consumers.

Reliable and resilient delivery
> At-least-once delivery of changes. We cannot tolerate the loss of a message, because it will completely mess up the data seen by downstream systems.

Message transformation support
> Should support lightweight message transformations because the event payload needs to match with the target system's input format.

Debezium

Debezium is an open source, distributed platform for change data capture, written by RedHat. It consists of a set of connectors that run in a Kafka Connect cluster. Each connector works with a specific database, where it captures changes as they occur and then streams a record of each change event to a topic in Kafka. These events are then read from the Kafka topic by consuming applications.

Debezium has connectors to read the change log of databases such as PostgreSQL, MySQL, MongoDB, Cassandra, and more. The source and sink connectors in Kafka Connect are used to get data out of source databases and into the target ones. Figure 7-4 shows how this works.

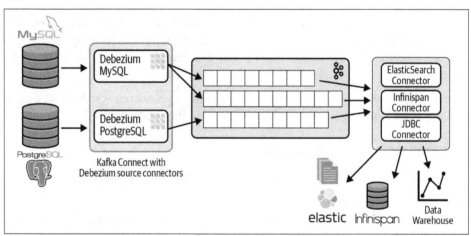

Figure 7-4. Debezium architecture

Now let's have a look at how we can use change data capture and Debezium at AATD.

Applying CDC to AATD

At the moment, our product catalogue is only stored in MySQL, but we need to make it accessible to the real-time analytics tooling. We're going to use Debezium to extract the product list from MySQL so that we can combine it with the orders stream to create an enriched order items stream. Doing this will make the data from our existing data infrastructure available to the real-time analytics tooling.

Figure 7-5 shows what we're going to build in this chapter.

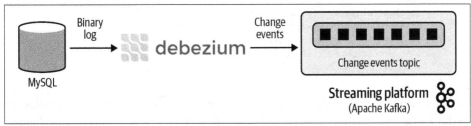

Figure 7-5. Streaming change events from MySQL to our streaming platform

Setup

The Docker Compose config for Debezium is defined in Example 7-1.

Example 7-1. docker-compose-pinot.yml

```
debezium:
  image: debezium/connect:1.8
  hostname: debezium
  container_name: debezium
  environment:
    BOOTSTRAP_SERVERS: kafka:9092
    GROUP_ID: 1
    CONFIG_STORAGE_TOPIC: connect_configs
    OFFSET_STORAGE_TOPIC: connect_offsets
  ports:
    - 8083:8083
  healthcheck: {test: curl -f localhost:8083, interval: 1s, start_period: 120s}
  depends_on:
    kafka: {condition: service_healthy}
    mysql: {condition: service_healthy}
```

Connecting Debezium to MySQL

Now we're going to connect Debezium to the `pizzashop` database in MySQL. We can do this by calling the HTTP endpoint for the MySQL connector:

```
curl -s -X PUT \
    -H "Content-Type:application/json" \
    http://localhost:8083/connectors/mysql/config \
    -d '{
    "connector.class": "io.debezium.connector.mysql.MySqlConnector",
    "database.hostname": "mysql",
    "database.port": 3306,
```

```
        "database.user": "debezium",
        "database.password": "dbz",
        "database.server.name": "mysql",
        "database.server.id": "223344",
        "database.allowPublicKeyRetrieval": true,
        "database.history.kafka.bootstrap.servers": "kafka:9092",
        "database.history.kafka.topic": "mysql-history",
        "database.include.list": "pizzashop",
        "time.precision.mode": "connect",
        "include.schema.changes": false
    }'
```

In this config, MySQL writes the change log for all tables in the `pizzashop` database to the Kafka broker running at `kafka:9092`. We aren't planning to make any changes to the schema, so we exclude schema changes from the published messages by setting the `include.schema.changes` property to `false`.

We can check that this has been configured correctly by calling the MySQL connector endpoint:

```
curl http://localhost:8083/connectors/mysql 2>/dev/null | jq '.'
```

If everything's working well, we should see something like the output in Example 7-2.

Example 7-2. MySQL connector config

```
{
  "name": "mysql",
  "config": {
    "connector.class": "io.debezium.connector.mysql.MySqlConnector",
    "database.allowPublicKeyRetrieval": "true",
    "database.user": "debezium",
    "database.server.id": "223344",
    "database.history.kafka.bootstrap.servers": "kafka:9092",
    "database.history.kafka.topic": "mysql-history",
    "time.precision.mode": "connect",
    "database.server.name": "mysql",
    "database.port": "3306",
    "include.schema.changes": "false",
    "database.hostname": "mysql",
    "database.password": "dbz",
    "name": "mysql",
    "database.include.list": "pizzashop"
  },
  "tasks": [
    {
      "connector": "mysql",
      "task": 0
    }
  ],
```

```
    "type": "source"
}
```

Querying the Products Stream

Debezium should now be populating events from MySQL's change log into the
`mysql.pizzashop.products` topic. Let's see if we have any data by running the following command, which returns the keys for one of the events in this stream:

```
kcat -C -b localhost:29092 -t mysql.pizzashop.products -c1 | jq 'keys'
```

We'll see the output in Example 7-3.

Example 7-3. Debezium products stream—keys

```
[
  "payload"
]
```

Each event has a `payload` that contains the data representing each record in MySQL.
These events will include any new products added to MySQL as well as changes to
existing records, such as updates to the product name, description, or price.

We can return the payload for one event by running the following command:

```
kcat -C -b localhost:29092 -t mysql.pizzashop.products -c1 | jq '.payload'
```

We can see the result of running this command in Example 7-4.

Example 7-4. Debezium products stream

```
{
  "before": null,
  "after": {
    "id": 1,
    "name": "Moroccan Spice Pasta Pizza - Veg",
    "description": "A pizza with a combination of Harissa sauce & delicious pasta.",
    "category": "veg pizzas",
    "price": 335,
    "image": "https://oreil.ly/LCGSv",
    "created_at": "2022-12-05T16:56:02Z",
    "updated_at": 1670259362000
  },
  "source": {
    "version": "1.8.1.Final",
    "connector": "mysql",
    "name": "mysql",
    "ts_ms": 1670259520651,
    "snapshot": "true",
    "db": "pizzashop",
```

```
    "sequence": null,
    "table": "products",
    "server_id": 0,
    "gtid": null,
    "file": "binlog.000002",
    "pos": 156,
    "row": 0,
    "thread": null,
    "query": null
  },
  "op": "r",
  "ts_ms": 1670259520668,
  "transaction": null
}
```

Looks good! We can see that each event has several top-level properties, including `before` and `after`, which represent a record before and after that change event. In this case, `before` is null, which means this event represents the creation of this record in the database.

Updating Products

At the moment, our `products` stream contains the values for each product from the initial ingestion that we did in "MySQL" on page 38. If updates are made to the `products` table, those changes will be picked up by Debezium as well.

Let's have a look at how that works by first connecting to the MySQL container:

```
docker exec -it mysql mysql -u mysqluser -p
```

Enter the password **mysqlpw** and then you'll see the `mysql` prompt.

We're going to change the name of the product with an `id` of 1, by running the following SQL query:

```
UPDATE pizzashop.products
SET name = 'Moroccan Spice Pasta Pizza'
WHERE id = 1;
```

You should see the following output:

```
Query OK, 1 row affected (0.00 sec)
Rows matched: 1  Changed: 1  Warnings: 0
```

One record has been changed, which Debezium will have picked up. Let's go back to the terminal and run the following command that filters the kcat output, using `jq`, to only show events with an `id` of 1:

```
kcat -C -b localhost:29092 -t mysql.pizzashop.products -u |
  jq '.payload | select(.after.id == 1) | {before, after}'
```

The output from running this command is shown in Example 7-5.

Example 7-5. Changing product name

```json
{
  "before": null,
  "after": {
    "id": 1,
    "name": "Moroccan Spice Pasta Pizza - Veg",
    "description": "A pizza with a combination of Harissa sauce & delicious pasta.",
    "category": "veg pizzas",
    "price": 335,
    "image": "https://oreil.ly/LCGSv",
    "created_at": "2022-12-05T16:56:02Z",
    "updated_at": 1670259362000
  }
}
{
  "before": {
    "id": 1,
    "name": "Moroccan Spice Pasta Pizza - Veg",
    "description": "A pizza with a combination of Harissa sauce & delicious pasta.",
    "category": "veg pizzas",
    "price": 335,
    "image": "https://oreil.ly/LCGSv",
    "created_at": "2022-12-05T16:56:02Z",
    "updated_at": 1670259362000
  },
  "after": {
    "id": 1,
    "name": "Moroccan Spice Pasta Pizza",
    "description": "A pizza with a combination of Harissa sauce & delicious pasta.",
    "category": "veg pizzas",
    "price": 335,
    "image": "https://oreil.ly/LCGSv",
    "created_at": "2022-12-05T16:56:02Z",
    "updated_at": 1670259897000
  }
}
```

It works! We have the initial entry when this product was added to the table, as well as the change that we just made. If we make any further changes to records in the products table, those will be written to `mysql.pizzashop.products` as well.

Summary

In this chapter, we learned about change data capture as a technique for making OLTP data available to a real-time analytics application. We then used Debezium to get product data out of MySQL and into the streaming platform.

Our products are now in Kafka and are ready to be joined with the orders. That's what we'll do in the next chapter.

CHAPTER 8

Joining Streams with Kafka Streams

Although the orders stream doesn't currently contain detailed information about products, in the last chapter we set up Debezium to capture any changes to the MySQL products table and write them into the products stream. In this chapter, you'll learn how to combine the orders stream and products streams by using a stream processor. We'll put the new stream into Apache Pinot and update the dashboard with the top-selling products and categories.

Enriching Orders with Kafka Streams

In Chapter 4, we used Kafka Streams to create a windowed aggregation over the orders stream so that we could compute the number of orders and revenue in the last few minutes. In this section, we're going to populate a new stream called enriched-order-items that will contain all the order items contained in the orders stream, hydrated with details from the products stream. Figure 8-1 shows what we're going to build in more detail.

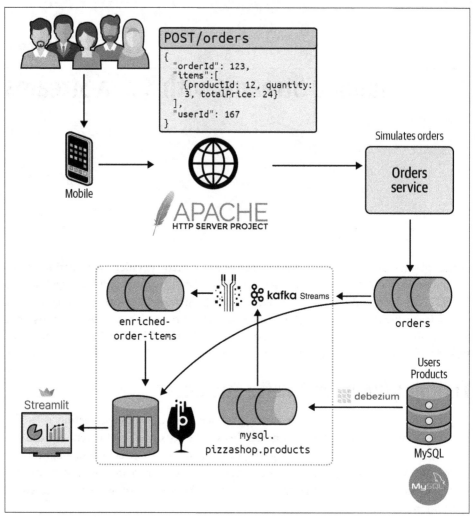

Figure 8-1. Architecture with enriched orders using Kafka Streams

We can break Figure 8-1 down further to visualize the different processors that will exist in the Kafka Streams graph to achieve this, as shown in Figure 8-2.

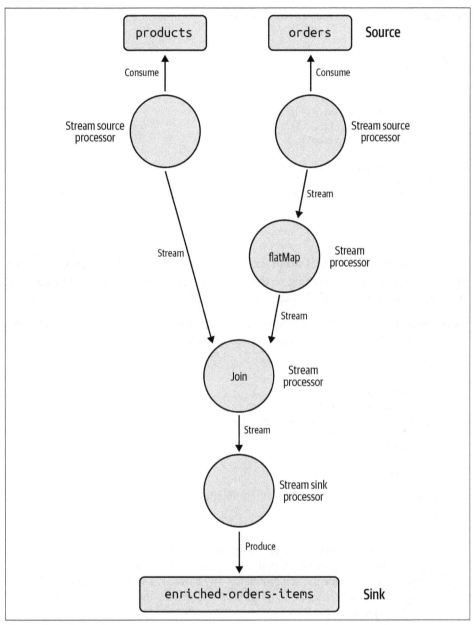

Figure 8-2. Kafka Streams processors

Now that we have an overview of what we're going to build, let's get to it. To recap, the product details that we're interested in are under the `payload` property, as shown in Example 8-1.

Example 8-1. Messages in the `products` *stream*

```json
{
  "payload": {
    "before": null,
    "after": {
      "id": 1,
      "name": "Moroccan Spice Pasta Pizza - Veg",
      "description": "A pizza with...",
      "category": "veg pizzas",
      "price": 335,
      "image": "https://oreil.ly/LCGSv",
      "created_at": "2022-12-05T16:56:02Z",
      "updated_at": 1670259362000
    }
  }
}
```

The `payload.after.id` in this event maps to the `productId` in the `items` of an order. We're going to ignore everything under `payload.before` since we're only interested in the updated order, not what change was made.

We're going to use serialization/deserialization code from Debezium to unpack these messages. Add the following dependency to the *pom.xml* file:

```xml
<dependencies>

    <dependency>
      <groupId>io.debezium</groupId>
      <artifactId>debezium-core</artifactId>
      <version>2.0.0.Final</version>
    </dependency>

<dependencies>
```

Next, let's have a look at the Kafka Streams code that creates the `enriched-order-items` stream.

 For brevity's sake, we are excluding all POJO (plain old Java object) and serialization/deserialization code from the examples. We also don't include the code to import any libraries, but you can find the full code sample (*https://oreil.ly/c7Pak*) in the book's GitHub repository.

Open the file *src/main/java/pizzashop/streams/Topology.java* that we created earlier. We're going to add to the topology that we created before.

Below the `orders` KStream, add a KTable over the `products` stream. This part of the code should look like this:

```
Serde<String> productKeySerde = DebeziumSerdes.payloadJson(String.class);
productKeySerde.configure(Collections.emptyMap(), true);

Serde<Product> productSerde = DebeziumSerdes.payloadJson(Product.class);
productSerde.configure(Collections.singletonMap("from.field", "after"), false);

KStream<String, Order> orders = builder.stream("orders",
    Consumed.with(Serdes.String(), orderSerde));

KTable<String, Product> products = builder.table(productsTopic,
    Consumed.with(productKeySerde, productSerde));
```

Next, create a stream of the order items in the `orders` stream keyed by `productId`:

```
KStream<String, OrderItemWithContext> orderItems = orders.flatMap(
  (key, value) -> {
    List<KeyValue<String, OrderItemWithContext>> result = new ArrayList<>();
    for (OrderItem item : value.items) {
        OrderItemWithContext orderItemWithContext = new OrderItemWithContext();
        orderItemWithContext.orderId = value.id;
        orderItemWithContext.orderItem = item;
        result.add(new
        KeyValue<>(String.valueOf(item.productId), orderItemWithContext));
    }
    return result;
});
```

We're using `productId` as the key for the new stream so that we can directly join it with the `products` KTable without needing to do a foreign-key join.

The `flatMap` method will flatten a list of streams or list of lists into one big stream, which is exactly what we need. Each order contains one or more order items, and we want to create a stream where each order item is its own event. Figure 8-3 uses an example order to illustrate what this bit of code does.

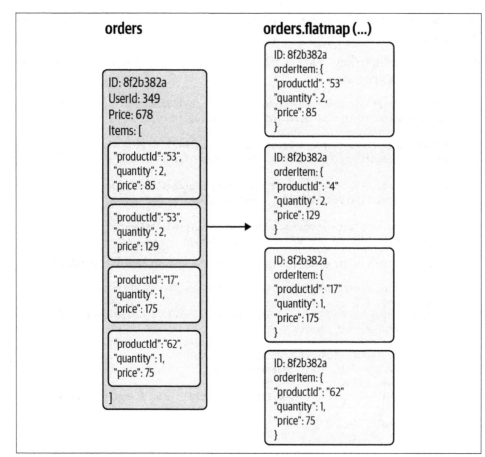

Figure 8-3. Extracting order items from orders

Under the hood, Kafka Streams will create a topic that contains the order items in this intermediate state. You might spot a reference to the name of this topic once we restart the Quarkus app.

> One thing to keep in mind when working with Kafka Streams is that, by default, to join records in two streams, they must have the same key. If they have different keys, the records won't be joined!

The next step is to enrich each of those order item events with their associated product. We can do this by joining `orderItems` and `products`:

```
KStream<String, HydratedOrderItem> hydratedOrderItems = orderItems.join(products,
    (orderItem, product) -> {
        HydratedOrderItem hydratedOrderItem = new HydratedOrderItem();
```

```
    hydratedOrderItem.orderId = orderItem.orderId;
    hydratedOrderItem.orderItem = orderItem.orderItem;
    hydratedOrderItem.product = product;
    return hydratedOrderItem;
});
```

Figure 8-4 provides a visual representation of what happens in this piece of code.

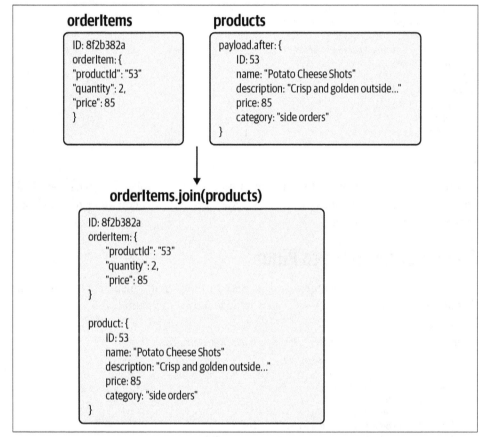

Figure 8-4. orderItems joined with products

Finally, let's write this new stream to the enriched-order-items topic:

```
hydratedOrderItems.to("enriched-order-items",
    Produced.with(Serdes.String(), hydratedOrderItemsSerde));
```

Our Quarkus app should automatically pick up these changes and start populating the enriched-order-items stream, which we can query with kcat:

```
kcat -C -b localhost:29092 -t enriched-order-items -c1 | jq '.'
```

You can see the output of running this command in Example 8-2.

Example 8-2. Messages in the `enriched-order-items` stream

```
{
  "orderId": "7bcd4bbe-c1a6-4bb3-807e-386a837bc2b3",
  "createdAt": "2022-09-13T05:22:53.617952",
  "product": {
    "id": "3",
    "name": "Pepsi Black Can",
    "description": "PEPSI BLACK CAN",
    "category": "beverages",
    "image": "https://oreil.ly/nYCzO",
    "price": 60
  },
  "orderItem": {
    "productId": "3",
    "quantity": 3,
    "price": 60
  }
}
```

If you don't see any events in this stream, it means that the join likely hasn't worked. You'll need to look at the logs of the `kafka-streams-quarkus` container to see if they indicate what's gone wrong.

Adding Order Items to Pinot

Next, we need to add a new table and schema to Pinot that consumes the data from this new stream. The schema for the new table is shown in Example 8-3.

Example 8-3. pinot/config/order_items_enriched/schema.json

```
{
  "schemaName": "order_items_enriched",
  "dimensionFieldSpecs": [
    {"name": "orderId", "dataType": "STRING"},
    {"name": "product.id", "dataType": "STRING"},
    {"name": "product.name", "dataType": "STRING"},
    {"name": "product.category", "dataType": "STRING"},
    {"name": "product.image", "dataType": "STRING"}
  ],
  "metricFieldSpecs": [
    {"name": "product.price", "dataType": "DOUBLE"},
    {"name": "orderItem.quantity", "dataType": "INT"}
  ],
  "dateTimeFieldSpecs": [
    {
      "name": "ts",
      "dataType": "TIMESTAMP",
      "format": "1:MILLISECONDS:EPOCH",
      "granularity": "1:MILLISECONDS"
```

```
      }
    ]
}
```

We could have flattened versions of these column names (e.g., id instead of product
.id, or category instead of product.category), but we'd need to write transformation functions for each column in the table config. For brevity's sake, we'll use the
nested column names, but this is something that you could change if you prefer to
have more concise column names.

The table config for order_items_enriched is shown in Example 8-4.

Example 8-4. pinot/config/order_items_enriched/table.json

```
{
  "tableName": "order_items_enriched",
  "tableType": "REALTIME",
  "segmentsConfig": {
    "timeColumnName": "ts",
    "timeType": "MILLISECONDS",
    "schemaName": "order_items_enriched",
    "replicasPerPartition": "1"
  },
  "tenants": {},
  "tableIndexConfig": {
    "loadMode": "MMAP",
    "streamConfigs": {
      "streamType": "kafka",
      "stream.kafka.consumer.type": "lowLevel",
      "stream.kafka.topic.name": "enriched-order-items",
      "stream.kafka.decoder.class.name":
        "org.apache.pinot.plugin.stream.kafka.KafkaJSONMessageDecoder",
      "stream.kafka.consumer.factory.class.name":
        "org.apache.pinot.plugin.stream.kafka20.KafkaConsumerFactory",
      "stream.kafka.broker.list": "kafka:9092",
      "stream.kafka.consumer.prop.auto.offset.reset": "smallest"
    }
  },
  "ingestionConfig": {
    "transformConfigs": [
      {
        "columnName": "ts",
        "transformFunction":
          "FromDateTime(\"createdAt\", 'yyyy-MM-dd''T''HH:mm:ss.SSSSSS')"
      }
    ]
  },
  "metadata": {"customConfigs": {}},
  "routing": {"instanceSelectorType": "strictReplicaGroup"}
}
```

The table config is similar to the one we saw for the orders table. The main differences are the table name, schema name, and that we're ingesting data from the enriched-order-items topic.

You can add this table and schema by running the following command:

```
docker run -v $PWD/pinot/config:/config \
  --network rta \
  apachepinot/pinot:0.10.0 \
  AddTable -schemaFile /config/order_items_enriched/schema.json \
          -tableConfigFile /config/order_items_enriched/table.json \
          -controllerHost pinot-controller \
          -exec
```

Once that's finished, open the Pinot Data Explorer (*http://localhost:9000*) and paste the following query in the query console:

```
select orderId,
       "product.name" AS name,
       "product.price" AS price,
       "product.category" AS category,
       "orderItem.quantity" AS quantity,
from order_items_enriched
limit 10
```

This query finds the first 10 items ingested from the enriched-order-items stream. You should see results similar to Table 8-1.

Table 8-1. Enriched order items

orderId	name	price	category	quantity
7bcd4bbe-c1a6-4bb3-807e-386a837bc2b3	Pepsi Black Can	60	beverages	3
7bcd4bbe-c1a6-4bb3-807e-386a837bc2b3	Cheese N Tomato	305	pizza mania	3
68916ba1-60c3-4567-b878-8723303760bf	Taco Mexicana Non Veg	175	side orders	1
68916ba1-60c3-4567-b878-8723303760bf	Spiced Double Chicken	569	chicken lovers pizza	2
68916ba1-60c3-4567-b878-8723303760bf	Veg Loaded	119	pizza mania	5
68916ba1-60c3-4567-b878-8723303760bf	Moroccan Spice Pasta Veg	145	pasta	4
ca1d03a3-7688-4397-b127-2e0726d03a03	The 5 Chicken Feast Pizza	709	chicken lovers pizza	1
ca1d03a3-7688-4397-b127-2e0726d03a03	Achari Do Pyaza	335	veg pizzas	1
ca1d03a3-7688-4397-b127-2e0726d03a03	Paneer & Onion	89	pizza mania	2
ca1d03a3-7688-4397-b127-2e0726d03a03	Indi Chicken Tikka	295	non veg pizzas	3

If you don't see any results, look at the Docker logs to see if there were any errors when ingesting the data into Pinot.

Updating the Orders Service

Now we need to make this data available via the orders service that we started building in Chapter 4. We'll want to show the best-selling products as well as the best-selling categories.

Let's start with an outline of the endpoint that we're going to create:

```
@GET
@Path("/popular")
public Response popular() {
    Map<String, Object> result = new HashMap<>();
    result.put("items", popularItems);
    result.put("categories", popularCategories);

    return Response.ok(result).build();
}
```

We're returning maps of `items` and `categories`, each of which will contain a list of five entries.

We can compute the most popular items sold in the last minute with the following SQL query:

```
SELECT "product.name" AS product,
       "product.image" AS image,
        distinctcount(orderId) AS orders,
        sum("orderItem.quantity") AS quantity
FROM order_items_enriched
where ts > ago('PT1M')
group by product, image
ORDER BY count(*) DESC
LIMIT 5
```

This query finds the top five items sold in the last minute. It returns the product name, image, number of orders, and quantity of items sold.

If we convert that query into Java, we end up with the following:

```
String itemQuery = DSL.using(SQLDialect.POSTGRES)
        .select(
                field("product.name").as("product"),
                field("product.image").as("image"),
                field("distinctcount(orderId)").as("orders"),
                sum(field("orderItem.quantity")
                    .coerce(Long.class)).as("quantity")
        )
        .from("order_items_enriched")
        .where(field("ts").greaterThan(field("ago('PT1M')")))
        .groupBy(field("product"), field("image"))
        .orderBy(field("count(*)").desc())
        .limit(DSL.inline(5))
        .getSQL();
```

```
ResultSet itemsResult = runQuery(connection, itemQuery);

List<PopularItem> popularItems = new ArrayList<>();
for (int index = 0; index < itemsResult.getRowCount(); index++) {
    popularItems.add(new PopularItem(
            itemsResult.getString(index, 0),
            itemsResult.getString(index, 1),
            itemsResult.getLong(index, 2),
            itemsResult.getDouble(index, 3)
    ));
}
```

This code also takes the query results and creates a list of `PopularItem` objects.

We can do the same for the popular categories with the following SQL query:

```
SELECT "product.category" AS category,
       distinctcount(orderId) AS orders,
       sum("orderItem.quantity") AS quantity
FROM order_items_enriched
where ts > ago('PT1M')
group by category
ORDER BY count(*) DESC
LIMIT 5
```

And in Java:

```
String categoryQuery = DSL.using(SQLDialect.POSTGRES)
        .select(
                field("product.category").as("category"),
                field("distinctcount(orderId)").as("orders"),
                sum(field("orderItem.quantity")
                    .coerce(Long.class)).as("quantity")
        )
        .from("order_items_enriched")
        .where(field("ts").greaterThan(field("ago('PT1M')")))
        .groupBy(field("category"))
        .orderBy(field("count(*)").desc())
        .limit(DSL.inline(5))
        .getSQL();

ResultSet categoryResult = runQuery(connection, categoryQuery);

List<PopularCategory> popularCategories = new ArrayList<>();
for (int index = 0; index < categoryResult.getRowCount(); index++) {
    popularCategories.add(new PopularCategory(
            categoryResult.getString(index, 0),
            categoryResult.getLong(index, 1),
            categoryResult.getDouble(index, 2)
    ));
}
```

The complete function for this endpoint looks like this:

```java
@GET
@Path("/popular")
public Response popular() {
    String itemQuery = DSL.using(SQLDialect.POSTGRES)
            .select(
                    field("product.name").as("product"),
                    field("product.image").as("image"),
                    field("distinctcount(orderId)").as("orders"),
                    sum(field("orderItem.quantity").
                        coerce(Long.class)).as("quantity")
            )
            .from("order_items_enriched")
            .where(field("ts").greaterThan(field("ago('PT1M')")))
            .groupBy(field("product"), field("image"))
            .orderBy(field("count(*)").desc())
            .limit(DSL.inline(5))
            .getSQL();

    ResultSet itemsResult = runQuery(connection, itemQuery);

    List<PopularItem> popularItems = new ArrayList<>();
    for (int index = 0; index < itemsResult.getRowCount(); index++) {
        popularItems.add(new PopularItem(
                itemsResult.getString(index, 0),
                itemsResult.getString(index, 1),
                itemsResult.getLong(index, 2),
                itemsResult.getDouble(index, 3)
        ));
    }

    String categoryQuery = DSL.using(SQLDialect.POSTGRES)
            .select(
                    field("product.category").as("category"),
                    field("distinctcount(orderId)").as("orders"),
                    sum(field("orderItem.quantity").
                        coerce(Long.class)).as("quantity")
            )
            .from("order_items_enriched")
            .where(field("ts").greaterThan(field("ago('PT1M')")))
            .groupBy(field("category"))
            .orderBy(field("count(*)").desc())
            .limit(DSL.inline(5))
            .getSQL();

    ResultSet categoryResult = runQuery(connection, categoryQuery);

    List<PopularCategory> popularCategories = new ArrayList<>();
    for (int index = 0; index < categoryResult.getRowCount(); index++) {
        popularCategories.add(new PopularCategory(
                categoryResult.getString(index, 0),
                categoryResult.getLong(index, 1),
                categoryResult.getDouble(index, 2)
```

```
      ));
    }

    Map<String, Object> result = new HashMap<>();
    result.put("items", popularItems);
    result.put("categories", popularCategories);

    return Response.ok(result).build();
  }
```

`PopularItem` and `PopularCategory` are both POJOs, so we won't show the code for those classes in the book.

Let's test whether the new endpoint is working by running the following command:

```
curl http://localhost:8080/orders/popular 2>/dev/null | jq '.'
```

We should see the output in Example 8-5.

Example 8-5. Popular items and category

```
{
  "categories": [
    {"category": "side orders", "orders": 680, "quantity": 3544},
    {"category": "veg pizzas", "orders": 581, "quantity": 2845},
    {"category": "pizza mania", "orders": 496, "quantity": 2295},
    {"category": "non veg pizzas", "orders": 501, "quantity": 2076},
    {"category": "pasta", "orders": 310, "quantity": 1122}
  ],
  "items": [
    {
      "product": "Creamy Tomato Pasta Non Veg",
      "image": "https://oreil.ly/grJT_",
      "orders": 87,
      "quantity": 257
    },
    {
      "product": "Veg Loaded",
      "image": "https://oreil.ly/iFOKN",
      "orders": 85,
      "quantity": 279
    },
    {
      "product": "Pepsi (500ml)",
      "image": "https://oreil.ly/hKB7K",
      "orders": 77,
      "quantity": 248
    },
    {
      "product": "Veggie Paradise",
      "image": "https://oreil.ly/Hyc11",
      "orders": 76,
```

```
      "quantity": 227
    },
    {
      "product": "Pepper Barbecue Chicken",
      "image": "https://oreil.ly/z8l4W",
      "orders": 78,
      "quantity": 214
    }
  ]
}
```

The API has been successfully updated, which leaves only the dashboard remaining.

Refreshing the Streamlit Dashboard

Now let's update our dashboard to show the top-selling items. We're going to create a table that displays the product, its image, and the number sold in a period of time. We'll use the functions in Example 8-6 to help render the data.

Example 8-6. Streamlit helper functions

```
def path_to_image_html(path):
    return '<img src="' + path + '" width="60" >'

@st.cache
def convert_df(input_df):
    return input_df.to_html(escape=False, formatters=dict(image=path_to_image_html))
```

Next, let's query the /orders/popular endpoint to get the most popular items and categories:

```
response = requests.get(f"{delivery_service_api}/orders/popular").json()
```

And now we'll add a section for the top-selling products. The code for this is in Example 8-7.

Example 8-7. Top-selling products

```
st.subheader("Most popular items")

popular_items = response["items"]
df = pd.DataFrame(popular_items)
df["quantityPerOrder"] = df["quantity"] / df["orders"]

html = convert_df(df)
st.markdown(html, unsafe_allow_html=True)
```

You can see the dashboard updated with this information in Figure 8-5.

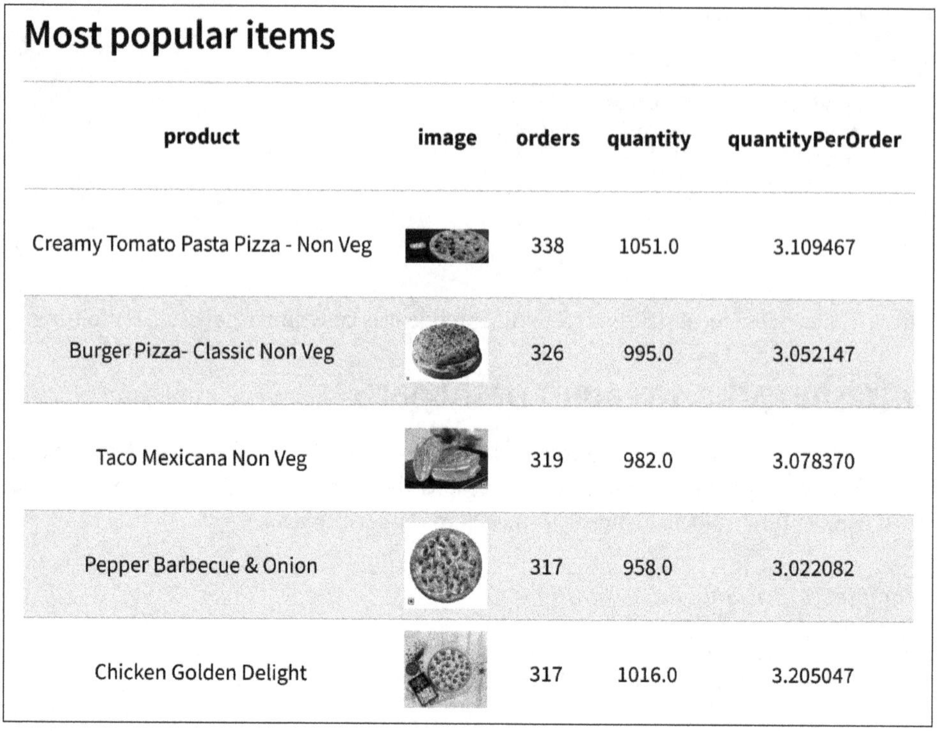

Most popular items

product	image	orders	quantity	quantityPerOrder
Creamy Tomato Pasta Pizza - Non Veg		338	1051.0	3.109467
Burger Pizza- Classic Non Veg		326	995.0	3.052147
Taco Mexicana Non Veg		319	982.0	3.078370
Pepper Barbecue & Onion		317	958.0	3.022082
Chicken Golden Delight		317	1016.0	3.205047

Figure 8-5. Top-selling products

Let's do the same for the top-selling product categories. The code to do this is shown in Example 8-8.

Example 8-8. Top-selling categories

```
st.subheader("Most popular categories")

popular_categories = response["categories"]
df = pd.DataFrame(popular_categories)
df["quantityPerOrder"] = df["quantity"] / df["orders"]

html = convert_df(df)
st.markdown(html, unsafe_allow_html=True)
```

You can see the updated dashboard in Figure 8-6.

Most popular categories

category	orders	quantity	quantityPerOrder
side orders	3240	17258.0	5.326543
veg pizzas	2955	14415.0	4.878173
non veg pizzas	2467	10858.0	4.401297
pizza mania	2482	10783.0	4.344480
pasta	1525	5612.0	3.680000

Figure 8-6. Top-selling categories

And on that delicious note, we're going to conclude the chapter!

Summary

In this chapter, we learned how to use Kafka Streams to join together the orders and products streams. Joining these streams of data made it possible to show the top-selling items and categories on our dashboard. In the next chapter, we're going to learn how to work with data whose state evolves over time.

CHAPTER 9

Upserts in the Serving Layer

AATD's operations team is happy with the progress we've made so far. They're now able to get real-time insights into popular products and categories, which is making procurement significantly easier.

But (and there's always a but, isn't there?), they've been receiving complaints about delayed orders, and at the moment, they don't have any insight into what's happening with the delivery of orders to customers. Customers would also like to know the status of their order and when it's likely to arrive at their residence.

In this chapter, we're going to solve both of those problems. We'll introduce order and delivery statuses, which will evolve over time. Working with this type of data will require the service to handle multiple events for the same order. In addition to wanting to know the latest status, we'll also want to know how that status has changed over time.

It's gonna be a fun chapter!

Order Statuses

As mentioned earlier, users want to be able to track the status of their order from when it's placed until it's delivered to them, and operators want to know if any orders aren't being fulfilled in a timely manner. To provide this functionality, we'll need to have order statuses.

We're going to add an `ordersStatuses` topic to Kafka to keep track of these states. Orders will go through the following stages:

- PLACED_ORDER
- ORDER_CONFIRMED
- BEING_PREPARED
- BEING_COOKED
- OUT_FOR_DELIVERY
- ARRIVING_AT_DOOR
- DELIVERED

In a real system, these status updates would be published by the service handling each stage. For example, the delivery service would take care of the OUT_FOR_DELIVERY, ARRIVING_AT_DOOR, and DELIVERED statuses.

This command outputs an example of how an order would move through the stages:

```
kcat -C -b localhost:29092 -t ordersStatuses |
  jq 'select(.id == "ed3fe5bc-2e2e-49c3-a2f3-367b4dd80000")'
```

The results are shown in Example 9-1.

Example 9-1. Order statuses from placement until delivery

```
{
  "id": "ed3fe5bc-2e2e-49c3-a2f3-367b4dd80000",
  "updatedAt": "2022-10-17T13:27:35.739917",
  "status": "PLACED_ORDER"
}
{
  "id": "ed3fe5bc-2e2e-49c3-a2f3-367b4dd80000",
  "updatedAt": "2022-10-17T13:30:07.739917",
  "status": "ORDER_CONFIRMED"
}
{
  "id": "ed3fe5bc-2e2e-49c3-a2f3-367b4dd80000",
  "updatedAt": "2022-10-17T13:30:20.739917",
  "status": "BEING_PREPARED"
}
{
  "id": "ed3fe5bc-2e2e-49c3-a2f3-367b4dd80000",
  "updatedAt": "2022-10-17T13:30:30.739917",
  "status": "BEING_COOKED"
}
{
  "id": "ed3fe5bc-2e2e-49c3-a2f3-367b4dd80000",
  "updatedAt": "2022-10-17T13:30:30.739917",
```

```
  "status": "OUT_FOR_DELIVERY"
}
{
  "id": "ed3fe5bc-2e2e-49c3-a2f3-367b4dd80000",
  "updatedAt": "2022-10-17T13:30:42.739917",
  "status": "ARRIVING_AT_DOOR"
}
{
  "id": "ed3fe5bc-2e2e-49c3-a2f3-367b4dd80000",
  "updatedAt": "2022-10-17T13:31:02.739917",
  "status": "DELIVERED"
}
```

Enriched Orders Stream

In addition to introducing the new ordersStatuses topic, we need to make some changes to the orders stream—it no longer needs to include a status field. Instead, we'll introduce a new enriched-orders stream that is populated based on a join of the orders and ordersStatuses streams. This will require an update to our Kafka Streams app.

This update means that the Kafka Streams application is now populating two different streams, as shown in Figure 9-1.

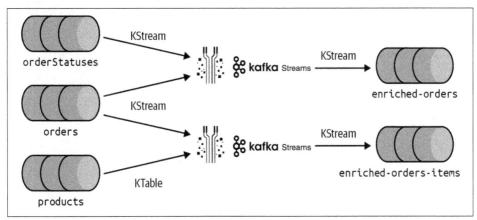

Figure 9-1. Kafka Streams app, joining, resulting in two enriched streams

Figure 9-2 shows in more detail what the new processors in our Kafka Streams topology are going to do.

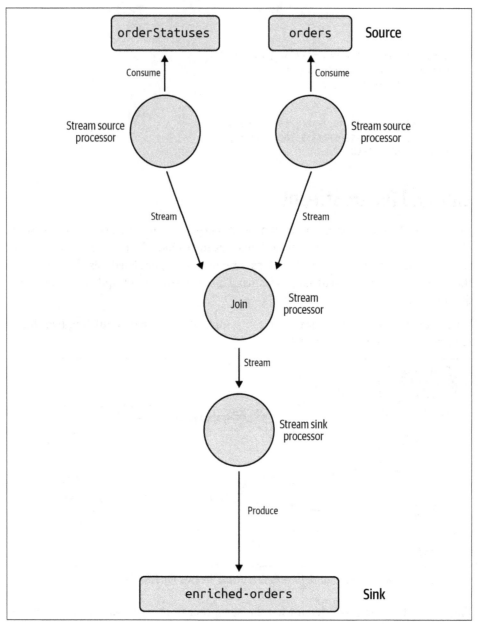

Figure 9-2. Joining `orders` and `orderStatuses`

Let's take a look at the code. We're going to revisit *src/main/java/pizzashop/streams/Topology.java* and add a couple of new topics to the top:

```
String orderStatusesTopic = System.getenv()
   .getOrDefault("ORDER_STATUSES_TOPIC", "ordersStatuses");
String enrichedOrdersTopic = System.getenv()
   .getOrDefault("ENRICHED_ORDERS_TOPIC", "enriched-orders");
```

Let's create a KStream around orderStatusesTopic:

```
KStream<String, OrderStatus> orderStatuses = builder.stream(orderStatusesTopic,
   Consumed.with(Serdes.String(), orderStatusSerde));
```

Finally, let's join orderStatuses with orders:

```
orders.join(orderStatuses, (value1, value2) -> {
         EnrichedOrder enrichedOrder = new EnrichedOrder();
         enrichedOrder.id = value1.id;
         enrichedOrder.items = value1.items;
         enrichedOrder.userId = value1.userId;
         enrichedOrder.status = value2.status;
         enrichedOrder.createdAt = value2.updatedAt;
         enrichedOrder.price = value1.price;
         return enrichedOrder;
      },
      JoinWindows.ofTimeDifferenceAndGrace(Duration.ofHours(2),
        Duration.ofHours(4)),
      StreamJoined.with(Serdes.String(), orderSerde, orderStatusSerde)
).to(enrichedOrdersTopic, Produced.with(Serdes.String(), enrichedOrdersSerde));
```

This code will publish events to the enriched-orders stream. We can see an example of the events for a single order by running the following:

```
kcat -C -b localhost:29092 -t enriched-orders |
jq -c 'select(.id == "ed3fe5bc-2e2e-49c3-a2f3-367b4dd80000") |
      {userId, createdAt, status, price}'
```

The results are shown in Example 9-2.

Example 9-2. Order statuses for one order

```
{"userId":"817","createdAt":"2022-10-17T13:27:35.739917",
  "status":"PLACED_ORDER","price":4259}
{"userId":"817","createdAt":"2022-10-17T13:30:07.739917",
  "status":"ORDER_CONFIRMED","price":4259}
{"userId":"817","createdAt":"2022-10-17T13:30:20.739917",
  "status":"BEING_PREPARED","price":4259}
{"userId":"817","createdAt":"2022-10-17T13:30:30.739917",
  "status":"BEING_COOKED","price":4259}
{"userId":"817","createdAt":"2022-10-17T13:30:37.739917",
  "status":"OUT_FOR_DELIVERY","price":4259}
{"userId":"817","createdAt":"2022-10-17T13:30:47.739917",
  "status":"ARRIVING_AT_DOOR","price":4259}
{"userId":"817","createdAt":"2022-10-17T13:31:12.739917",
  "status":"DELIVERED","price":4259}
```

This order only took four minutes to be delivered from the time it was ordered! Obviously, real-life orders would take a bit longer, but it's good that the order is making it all the way through the system—everything is working as expected.

We'll also need to create a new table in Apache Pinot that can deal with multiple events that have the same order ID.

Upserts in Apache Pinot

Pinot provides native support for *upserts*, which we can use to handle the evolution of the order status. To enable this functionality, we need to specify a primary key, which in this case will be the order ID. When we query our table, Pinot will only return the most recent event for that order ID. This will be helpful for working out the latest state of an order.

Sometimes we might want to see the history of those order statuses, though; for example, we might want to see how long orders are taking to get through each step. Pinot can handle this use case as well, via a query flag. Pinot still keeps a copy of all the events ingested from the streaming platform; the upsert functionality is just an abstraction layer on top of this.

We can't retrospectively add upsert support to a table that already contains data, so we're going to create a new table. The new table is called orders_enriched, and its config is defined in Example 9-3.

Example 9-3. pinot/config/orders_enriched/table.json

```
{
    "tableName": "orders_enriched",
    "tableType": "REALTIME",
    "segmentsConfig": {
      "timeColumnName": "ts",
      "timeType": "MILLISECONDS",
      "retentionTimeUnit": "DAYS",
      "retentionTimeValue": "1",
      "schemaName": "orders_enriched",
      "replicasPerPartition": "1"
    },
    "upsertConfig": {"mode": "FULL"},
    "tenants": {},
    "tableIndexConfig": {
      "loadMode": "MMAP",
      "streamConfigs": {
        "streamType": "kafka",
        "stream.kafka.consumer.type": "lowLevel",
        "stream.kafka.topic.name": "enriched-orders",
        "stream.kafka.decoder.class.name":
          "org.apache.pinot.plugin.stream.kafka.KafkaJSONMessageDecoder",
```

```
        "stream.kafka.consumer.factory.class.name":
          "org.apache.pinot.plugin.stream.kafka20.KafkaConsumerFactory",
        "stream.kafka.broker.list": "kafka:9092",
        "stream.kafka.consumer.prop.auto.offset.reset": "smallest"
      }
    },
    "ingestionConfig": {
      "complexTypeConfig": {"delimiter": "."},
      "transformConfigs": [
        {
          "columnName": "ts",
          "transformFunction":
            "FromDateTime(\"createdAt\", 'yyyy-MM-dd''T''HH:mm:ss.SSSSSS')"
        }
      ]
    },
    "metadata": {"customConfigs": {}},
    "routing": {"instanceSelectorType": "strictReplicaGroup"}
}
```

This code makes a couple of changes to the table config that we saw in Example 5-4:

- `stream.kafka.topic.name` is now `enriched-orders` instead of `orders`.
- `segmentsConfig.schemaName` and `tableName` are now `orders_enriched` instead of `orders`.

We've also added the following config to enable upserts:

```
"upsertConfig": {"mode": "FULL"}
```

Everything else remains the same.

 Pinot supports two types of upsert: full and partial. Full means that, for a given primary key, a new record will completely replace the older record. Partial means that, for a given primary key, you can configure a strategy for each field.

You can read more about these strategies (*https://oreil.ly/aldW7*) in the Pinot documentation.

Next, it's time to look at the schema for our new table, which is described in Example 9-4.

Example 9-4. pinot/config/orders_enriched/schema.json

```
{
    "schemaName": "orders_enriched",
    "primaryKeyColumns": ["id"],
    "dimensionFieldSpecs": [
```

```
      {"name": "id", "dataType": "STRING"},
      {"name": "userId", "dataType": "INT"},
      {"name": "status", "dataType": "STRING"},
      {"name": "items", "dataType": "JSON"}
    ],
    "metricFieldSpecs": [{"name": "price", "dataType": "DOUBLE"}],
    "dateTimeFieldSpecs": [
      {
        "name": "ts",
        "dataType": "TIMESTAMP",
        "format": "1:MILLISECONDS:EPOCH",
        "granularity": "1:MILLISECONDS"
      }
    ]
  }
```

When we're defining the schema for an upserts table, we need to define the `primary KeyColumns` property. We can provide multiple column names if our events are identified via a composite key, but in our case, events can be uniquely identified by the `id` property.

We'll create this table by running the following:

```
docker run -v $PWD/pinot/config:/config \
  --network rta \
  apachepinot/pinot:0.11.0-arm64 \
  AddTable -schemaFile /config/orders_enriched/schema.json \
          -tableConfigFile /config/orders_enriched/table.json \
          -controllerHost pinot-controller \
          -exec
```

Once we've done that, let's navigate to the Pinot Data Explorer and query the new table:

```
select id, userId, status, price, ts
from orders_enriched
limit 10
```

We should see something like the output in Table 9-1.

Table 9-1. Querying the orders_enriched table

id	userId	status	price	ts
816b9d84-9426-4055-9d48-54d11496bfbe	1046	DELIVERED	4206	2022-12-08 12:03:49.768
d06545bb-48ef-4e0a-8d7f-e2916cef2508	7269	DELIVERED	7572	2022-12-08 12:03:51.612
a14ff1d9-59d7-456e-a205-37faf274145d	9123	DELIVERED	2423	2022-12-08 12:03:55.396
de283949-76a3-4898-ac3e-0bd8bc9ab0bc	5376	DELIVERED	580	2022-12-08 12:04:04.036
08309572-4b20-42a6-8cc7-340b42f636ae	1637	DELIVERED	1622	2022-12-08 12:04:10.126
f45eb73f-c38d-4176-9233-54bb62ec2716	7467	DELIVERED	2672	2022-12-08 12:04:11.206
d8bb71a6-e23e-483e-9687-6c7da0da2a62	1046	DELIVERED	9439	2022-12-08 12:04:13.111

id	userId	status	price	ts
2d115b4d-efe6-4988-a04b-fe78e3536ff9	6990	DELIVERED	6116	2022-12-08 12:04:15.278
0c70239e-5bd0-4e83-b59c-00832796c848	2820	OUT_FOR_DELIVERY	3646	2022-12-08 12:04:18.917
3931d15b-f99a-43ea-8d62-5fcaceba64b5	288	DELIVERED	814	2022-12-08 12:04:20.659

We could also choose a specific id and then run the following query to see all the states that it's gone through:

```
select id, userId, status, price, ts
from orders_enriched
WHERE id = '816b9d84-9426-4055-9d48-54d11496bfbe'
limit 10
option(skipUpsert=true)
```

We're using the skipUpsert=true flag to tell Pinot to return all the records associated with this id rather than just the latest one, which is what it would do by default.

The results of that query are shown in Table 9-2.

Table 9-2. All the statuses for order 816b9d84-9426-4055-9d48-54d11496bfbe

id	userId	status	price	ts
816b9d84-9426-4055-9d48-54d11496bfbe	1046	PLACED_ORDER	4206	2022-12-08 12:02:47.386
816b9d84-9426-4055-9d48-54d11496bfbe	1046	ORDER_CONFIRMED	4206	2022-12-08 12:03:02.386
816b9d84-9426-4055-9d48-54d11496bfbe	1046	BEING_PREPARED	4206	2022-12-08 12:03:14.386
816b9d84-9426-4055-9d48-54d11496bfbe	1046	BEING_COOKED	4206	2022-12-08 12:03:27.386
816b9d84-9426-4055-9d48-54d11496bfbe	1046	OUT_FOR_DELIVERY	4206	2022-12-08 12:03:46.386
816b9d84-9426-4055-9d48-54d11496bfbe	1046	ARRIVING_AT_DOOR	4206	2022-12-08 12:03:48.768
816b9d84-9426-4055-9d48-54d11496bfbe	1046	DELIVERED	4206	2022-12-08 12:03:49.768

Updating the Orders Service

Next we need to add some endpoints to the orders service. The frontend app needs to retrieve the latest status as well as previous statuses for an order ID. We also need to be able to get a list of orders for a specific user ID.

We'll add the following endpoints:

/orders/<order-id>
    Returns all the statuses for an order

/users/*<user-id>*/orders
> Returns all the orders for a user

/users
> Returns a list of users. This endpoint is needed so that we can include a list of users in our app and then analyze the orders for different people.

We'll add these endpoints to the Quarkus application that we've been building. Our endpoints will need to query the backend Pinot database and then massage the response into the formats described previously.

Creating UsersResource

Now we're going to create a new file, */src/main/java/pizzashop/rest/UsersResource.java*. We'll start with the following shell:

```
@ApplicationScoped
@Path("/users")
public class UsersResource {
    private Connection connection = ConnectionFactory.fromHostList(
        System.getenv().getOrDefault("PINOT_BROKER", "localhost:8099"));

    private static ResultSet runQuery(Connection connection, String query) {
        ResultSetGroup resultSetGroup = connection.execute(query);
        return resultSetGroup.getResultSet(0);
    }
}
```

Adding an allUsers Endpoint

We'll start with the /users endpoint, which returns a list of users. The data will be in the following format:

```
[
    {"userId": "<userId1>", "name": "<userName1>"},
    {"userId": "<userId2>", "name": "<userName2>"}
]
```

Add the following function for this endpoint:

```
@GET
@Path("/")
public Response allUsers() {
    String query = DSL.using(SQLDialect.POSTGRES)
            .select(field("userId"), field("ts"))
            .from("orders")
            .orderBy(field("ts").desc())
            .limit(DSL.inline(50))
            .getSQL();

    ResultSet resultSet = runQuery(connection, query);
```

```
Stream<Map<String, Object>> rows = IntStream.range(
    0, resultSet.getRowCount()).mapToObj(
        index -> Map.of("userId", resultSet.getString(index, 0)));

    return Response.ok(rows).build();
}
```

We can test out this endpoint by running the following command:

```
curl http://localhost:8080/users 2>/dev/null | jq -c '.[]' | head -n5
```

The results are shown in Example 9-5.

Example 9-5. Five random users

```
{"userId":"2480"}
{"userId":"8589"}
{"userId":"2233"}
{"userId":"7028"}
{"userId":"1677"}
```

Adding an Orders for User Endpoint

Next, we have the */users/<user-id>/orders* endpoint. The data returned will be in the following format:

```
[
    {"id": "<orderid1>", "price": "<price1>", "ts": "<ts1>"},
    {"id": "<orderid2>", "price": "<price2>", "ts": "<ts2>"}
]
```

Add the following code:

```
@GET
@Path("/{userId}/orders")
public Response userOrders(@PathParam("userId") String userId) {
    String query = DSL.using(SQLDialect.POSTGRES)
            .select(
                    field("id"),
                    field("price"),
                    field("ToDateTime(ts, 'YYYY-MM-dd HH:mm:ss')").as("ts")
            )
            .from("orders_enriched")
            .where(field("userId").eq(field("'" + userId + "'")))
            .orderBy(field("ts").desc())
            .limit(DSL.inline(50))
            .getSQL();

    ResultSet resultSet = runQuery(connection, query);

    List<Map<String, Object>> rows = new ArrayList<>();
    for (int index = 0; index < resultSet.getRowCount(); index++) {
```

```
        rows.add(Map.of(
                "id", resultSet.getString(index, 0),
                "price", resultSet.getDouble(index, 1),
                "ts", resultSet.getString(index, 2)
        ));
    }

    return Response.ok(rows).build();
}
```

The query used in this function finds the most recent 50 orders for a given user. We can test it out by running the following command:

```
curl http://localhost:8080/users/2491/orders 2>/dev/null | jq -c '.[]' | head -n5
```

The results are shown in Example 9-6.

Example 9-6. The orders for user 2491

```
{"ts":"2022-12-09 13:35:31","price":2419,"id":"d84ecc16-a60c-4856-ba2c-fd5879a6f57c"}
{"ts":"2022-12-09 13:34:14","price":5127,"id":"4e62cac8-db2c-4382-8ef9-22dfb511d94b"}
{"ts":"2022-12-09 13:28:58","price":6695,"id":"0fb9a8f2-d8fa-40b6-9933-32b44f99eb68"}
{"ts":"2022-12-09 13:26:09","price":4685,"id":"d8ef57d0-8522-4a0a-94ad-e4bcc6af2ee2"}
{"ts":"2022-12-09 13:15:54","price":1800,"id":"e8174f81-1867-4981-9270-b7a530e24f17"}
```

Adding an Individual Order Endpoint

Finally, we're going to implement the /orders/*<order-id>* endpoint. The data returned will be in the following format:

```
[
    "userId": "<userId>",
    "statuses": [
        {"ts":"<ts1>","status":"<status1>"}
    ],
    "products": [
        {
            "image": "<image>",
            "price": "<price>",
            "product": "<product>",
            "quantity": "<quantity>"
        }
    ]
]
```

The code for this endpoint will live in OrdersResource, so let's open that file again. This endpoint needs to bring together the results of three different queries that retrieve the user, products, and statuses for a given order.

The code is shown here:

```
@GET
@Path("/{orderId}")
public Response order(@PathParam("orderId") String orderId) {
    // Get user
    String userQuery = DSL.using(SQLDialect.POSTGRES)
            .select(field("userId"))
            .from("orders")
            .where(field("id").eq(field("'" + orderId + "'")))
            .getSQL();
    ResultSet userResultSet = runQuery(connection, userQuery);
    Stream<String> userIds = IntStream.range(0, userResultSet.getRowCount())
            .mapToObj(index -> userResultSet.getString(index, 0));

    // Get list of products
    String productsQuery = DSL.using(SQLDialect.POSTGRES)
            .select(
                    field("product.name").as("product"),
                    field("product.price").as("price"),
                    field("product.image").as("image"),
                    field("orderItem.quantity").as("quantity")
            )
            .from("order_items_enriched")
            .where(field("orderId").eq(field("'" + orderId + "'")))
            .getSQL();
    ResultSet productsResultSet = runQuery(connection, productsQuery);
    Stream<Map<String, Object>> products = IntStream.range(0,
            productsResultSet.getRowCount())
            .mapToObj(index -> Map.of(
                    "product", productsResultSet.getString(index, 0),
                    "price", productsResultSet.getDouble(index, 1),
                    "image", productsResultSet.getString(index, 2),
                    "quantity", productsResultSet.getLong(index, 3)
            ));

    // Get list of statuses
    String statusesQuery = DSL.using(SQLDialect.POSTGRES)
            .select(
                    field("ToDateTime(ts, 'YYYY-MM-dd HH:mm:ss')").as("ts"),
                    field("status"),
                    field("userId").as("image")
            )
            .from("orders_enriched")
            .where(field("id").eq(field("'" + orderId + "'")))
            .orderBy(field("ts").desc())
            .option("option(skipUpsert=true)")
            .getSQL();
    ResultSet statusesResultSet = runQuery(connection, statusesQuery);
    Stream<Map<String, Object>> statuses = IntStream.range(0,
            statusesResultSet.getRowCount())
            .mapToObj(index -> Map.of(
                    "timestamp", statusesResultSet.getString(index, 0),
                    "status", statusesResultSet.getString(index, 1)
```

```
            ));

        return Response.ok(Map.of(
                "userId", userIds.findFirst().orElse(""),
                "products", products,
                "statuses", statuses
        )).build();
    }
```

We can test it out by running the following command:

```
id="f16f61be-a082-478c-a781-39bc69d174dc"
curl http://localhost:8080/orders/${id} 2> /dev/null | jq '.'
```

The results of this command are shown in Example 9-7.

Example 9-7. The details for order f16f61be-a082-478c-a781-39bc69d174dc

```
{
  "products": [
    {
      "price": 185,
      "product": "Boneless Chicken Wings Peri-peri",
      "quantity": 3,
      "image": "https://oreil.ly/_zoSw"
    },
    {
      "price": 149,
      "product": "Burger Pizza- Premium Veg",
      "quantity": 5,
      "image": "https://oreil.ly/x1aer"
    },
    {
      "price": 89,
      "product": "Paneer & Onion",
      "quantity": 3,
      "image": "https://oreil.ly/1Nq2V"
    }
  ],
  "userId": "929",
  "statuses": [
    {
      "status": "DELIVERED",
      "timestamp": "2022-12-08 18:06:33"
    },
    {
      "status": "ARRIVING_AT_DOOR",
      "timestamp": "2022-12-08 18:04:33"
    },
    {
      "status": "OUT_FOR_DELIVERY",
      "timestamp": "2022-12-08 18:03:43"
```

```
  },
  {
    "status": "BEING_COOKED",
    "timestamp": "2022-12-08 18:03:01"
  },
  {
    "status": "BEING_PREPARED",
    "timestamp": "2022-12-08 18:02:49"
  },
  {
    "status": "ORDER_CONFIRMED",
    "timestamp": "2022-12-08 18:02:39"
  },
  {
    "status": "PLACED_ORDER",
    "timestamp": "2022-12-08 18:02:11"
  }
 ]
}
```

This particular order has already been delivered, so we can see every status. When an order is still in progress, we'll only see some of these statuses in the result.

Configuring Cross-Origin Resource Sharing

We'll also need to configure cross-origin resource sharing (CORS) in the Quarkus app's `application.properties` so that can we call the endpoints via an XML HTTP request from our frontend application. Add the following properties:

```
quarkus.http.cors=true
quarkus.http.cors.origins=http://localhost:3000
quarkus.http.cors.headers=accept, authorization, content-type, x-requested-with
quarkus.http.cors.methods=GET, OPTIONS
```

> This config assumes that our frontend application is deployed to *http://localhost:3000*. We'd need to update `quarkus.http.cors.origins` to handle a different location.

Frontend App

We're going to create a basic React application using Next.js (*https://nextjs.org*) and the Material UI toolkit (*https://mui.com*). The application will let us simulate viewing the orders for an individual user, which we'll select on the first page.

Figure 9-3 shows which endpoints provide data to the frontend pages.

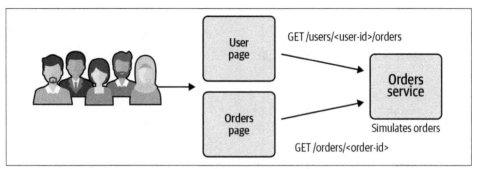

Figure 9-3. Data flow from the orders service to end users

We won't go into the code details of this app, but you can find everything in the book's GitHub repository.

Let's still have a look at some screenshots of the pages. In Figure 9-4, you can see the user page.

Orders for user 414

REFRESH ORDERS

| 2022-10-21 14:49:25 | ff240208-5f2f-4edd-baac-a6c60c61f11d | 3547₹ | VIEW ORDER |

| 2022-10-21 14:51:58 | 17e1466f-4987-4203-8ae9-5de4056f8cf6 | 145₹ | VIEW ORDER |

| 2022-10-21 14:56:38 | 3cb2c388-a3f8-4fe3-ae3c-a590ab6f7e63 | 7502₹ | VIEW ORDER |

| 2022-10-21 14:59:12 | 9d5920c4-cd48-4ea1-b369-16803ebc07f5 | 4131₹ | VIEW ORDER |

| 2022-10-21 15:01:04 | cbc0d228-57c5-44e5-8a02-a98d54d8dbec | 435₹ | VIEW ORDER |

Figure 9-4. User page

And if we click one of those orders, we'll see Figure 9-5.

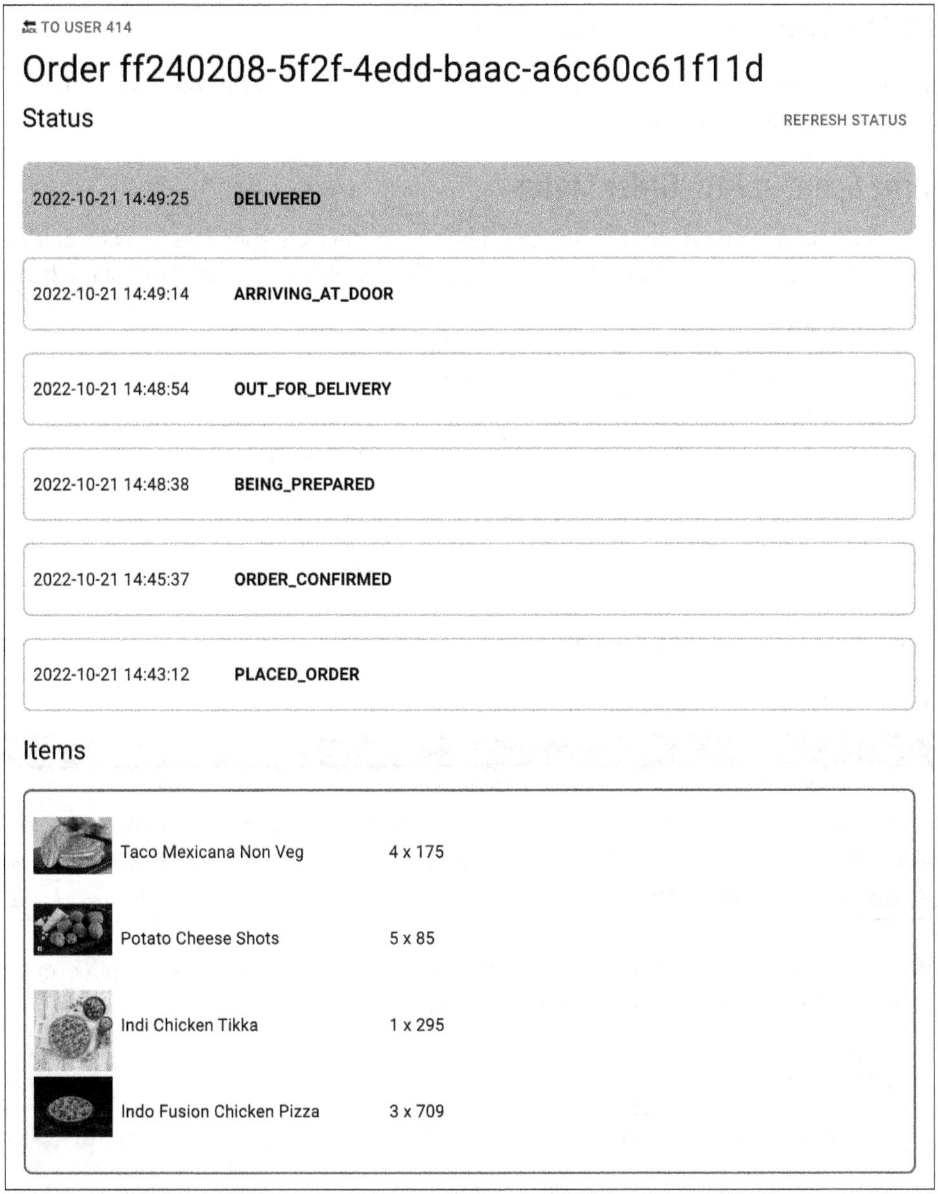

Order ff240208-5f2f-4edd-baac-a6c60c61f11d

Status

REFRESH STATUS

2022-10-21 14:49:25	**DELIVERED**

2022-10-21 14:49:14	**ARRIVING_AT_DOOR**

2022-10-21 14:48:54	**OUT_FOR_DELIVERY**

2022-10-21 14:48:38	**BEING_PREPARED**

2022-10-21 14:45:37	**ORDER_CONFIRMED**

2022-10-21 14:43:12	**PLACED_ORDER**

Items

	Taco Mexicana Non Veg	4 x 175
	Potato Cheese Shots	5 x 85
	Indi Chicken Tikka	1 x 295
	Indo Fusion Chicken Pizza	3 x 709

Figure 9-5. Statuses from order placement to delivery

The user can click the Refresh Status link to make a background request to the orders service, which will return the latest status.

Order Statuses on the Dashboard

We also want to be able to track statuses on the dashboard, but this time we're interested in them as an aggregate.

Time Spent in Each Order Status

For example, we might want to see the time that orders are spending in each status. The following query computes various percentiles for orders currently in the kitchen:

```
select status,
          min((now() - ts) / 1000) as min,
          percentile((now() - ts) / 1000, 50) AS percentile50,
       avg((now() - ts) / 1000) as avg,
          percentile((now() - ts) / 1000, 75) AS percentile75,
          percentile((now() - ts) / 1000, 90) AS percentile90,
          percentile((now() - ts) / 1000, 90) AS percentile99,
       max((now() - ts) / 1000) as max
from orders_enriched
WHERE status NOT IN ('DELIVERED', 'OUT_FOR_DELIVERY')
group by status;
```

You should see something like the output in Table 9-3.

Table 9-3. Percentiles for different order statuses

status	min	percentile50	avg	percentile75	percentile90	percentile99	max
ORDER_CONFIRMED	18.723	22.935	23.13713333333334	25.452	27.114	29.13	29.719
BEING_COOKED	18.752	38.39	39.55397026604069	47.026	60.505	72.908	77.366
BEING_PREPARED	18.715	25.705	25.971310344827568	29.753	32.114	35.277	35.526
PLACED_ORDER	14.544	25.708	26.718140921409194	32.268	38.268	46.308	47.852

We can update `OrdersResource` in the orders service to have a new endpoint, `/orders/statuses`, that returns this data:

```
@GET
@Path("/statuses")
public Response statuses() {
    String query = DSL.using(SQLDialect.POSTGRES)
          .select(
                field("status"),
                min(field("(now() - ts) / 1000")),
                field("percentile((now() - ts) / 1000, 50)"),
                avg(field("(now() - ts) / 1000").coerce(Long.class)),
                field("percentile((now() - ts) / 1000, 75)"),
                field("percentile((now() - ts) / 1000, 90)"),
                field("percentile((now() - ts) / 1000, 99)"),
                max(field("(now() - ts) / 1000"))
          )
```

```
                    .from("orders_enriched")
                    .where(field("status NOT IN ('DELIVERED', 'OUT_FOR_DELIVERY')")
                        .coerce(Boolean.class))
                    .groupBy(field("status"))
                    .getSQL();

        ResultSet resultSet = runQuery(connection, query);

        List<Map<String, Object>> rows = new ArrayList<>();
        for (int index = 0; index < resultSet.getRowCount(); index++) {
            rows.add(Map.of(
                    "status", resultSet.getString(index, 0),
                    "min", resultSet.getDouble(index, 1),
                    "percentile50", resultSet.getDouble(index, 2),
                    "avg", resultSet.getDouble(index, 3),
                    "percentile75", resultSet.getDouble(index, 4),
                    "percentile90", resultSet.getDouble(index, 5),
                    "percentile99", resultSet.getDouble(index, 6),
                    "max", resultSet.getDouble(index, 7)
            ));
        }

        return Response.ok(rows).build();
    }
```

We can test it out by running the following command:

```
curl http://localhost:8080/orders/statuses 2>/dev/null | \
    jq '.[] | {status, min, percentile50, max}'
```

The results are shown in Example 9-8.

Example 9-8. Order statuses

```
{
  "status": "ORDER_CONFIRMED",
  "min": 26.15,
  "percentile50": 30.587,
  "max": 38.136
}
{
  "status": "BEING_COOKED",
  "min": 26.21,
  "percentile50": 44.871,
  "max": 82.065
}
{
  "status": "BEING_PREPARED",
  "min": 26.213,
  "percentile50": 32.892,
  "max": 43.522
}
```

```
{
  "status": "PLACED_ORDER",
  "min": 21.254,
  "percentile50": 33.066,
  "max": 55.024
}
```

We could then update the dashboard to include the data from this endpoint. The following code calls the new endpoint and renders the results in a DataFrame:

```
st.subheader("Order Statuses Overview")

popular_items = requests.get(f"{delivery_service_api}/orders/statuses").json()
df = pd.DataFrame(popular_items)[[
    "status", "min", "avg", "percentile50", "percentile75",
    "percentile90", "percentile99", "max"
]]

html = convert_df(df)
st.markdown(html, unsafe_allow_html=True)
```

We can see a screenshot in Figure 9-6.

Order Statuses Overview

status	min	avg	percentile50	percentile75	percentile90	percentile99	max
ORDER_CONFIRMED	9.092	14.236254	14.345	16.756	18.693	20.150	20.150
BEING_COOKED	9.105	31.573907	29.921	41.360	52.272	65.674	67.913
BEING_PREPARED	9.135	17.771280	18.061	21.233	23.633	25.806	25.948
PLACED_ORDER	0.198	15.793795	15.626	23.452	28.501	34.528	37.860

Figure 9-6. An overview of order statuses

Orders That Might Be Stuck

Knowing those percentiles is interesting, but our operators can't take action on that data. To take action, we need to know which specific orders might be delayed.

The operators have actually observed that orders are most often getting stuck in the BEING_COOKED status. We can write the following query to find the orders that have been in this status for more than 60 seconds:

```
select id, price, ts, (now() - ts) / 1000 AS timeInStatus
from orders_enriched
WHERE status = 'BEING_COOKED'
AND (now() - ts) > 60787
ORDER BY ts
LIMIT 10
```

You should see something like the output in Table 9-4.

Table 9-4. Orders stuck in the BEING_COOKED status for a while

id	price	ts	timeInStatus
5dfd4a75-75df-4a27-93d8-e340afbea98f	75	2022-12-12 13:37:59.64	64.413
f1df8c67-8de9-4ee1-a5de-1243da507351	5405	2022-12-12 13:37:59.941	64.112
8fb205ac-8b43-4415-ad0f-910191f2eab9	5153	2022-12-12 13:38:00.897	63.156
d6e6efcb-9079-40b3-949e-50a48a796f6d	3870	2022-12-12 13:38:01.443	62.61
011884fe-1d6a-48ec-a30d-a7742ed76aad	915	2022-12-12 13:38:02.497	61.556
1fd992fa-bec8-4059-a503-39c72c02e31d	2012	2022-12-12 13:38:02.612	61.441
e78ba33a-4396-4de8-85d9-8560bce2fdf3	2403	2022-12-12 13:38:02.798	61.255
85df8d71-322a-434e-ab4b-11724b0568a8	7156	2022-12-12 13:38:03.004	61.049
9bc6ed4f-246b-471a-a280-b5d3f67c856d	1876	2022-12-12 13:38:03.158	60.895
71fd27a8-4fc9-4c50-a30d-cbfc327c1205	848	2022-12-12 13:38:03.231	60.822

We can update OrdersResource in the orders service to have a new endpoint, /orders/stuck/<orderStatus>/<stuckTimeInMillis>, that returns this data:

```
@GET
@Path("/stuck/{orderStatus}/{stuckTimeInMillis}")
public Response stuckOrders(
        @PathParam("orderStatus") String orderStatus,
        @PathParam("stuckTimeInMillis") Long stuckTimeInMillis
) {
    String query = DSL.using(SQLDialect.POSTGRES)
            .select(
                    field("id"),
                    field("price"),
                    field("ts"),
                    field("(now() - ts) / 1000")
            )
            .from("orders_enriched")
            .where(field("status").eq(field("'" + orderStatus + "'")))
            .and(field("(now() - ts) > " + stuckTimeInMillis)
            .coerce(Boolean.class))
            .orderBy(field("ts"))
```

```
            .getSQL();

        ResultSet resultSet = runQuery(connection, query);

        List<Map<String, Object>> rows = new ArrayList<>();
        for (int index = 0; index < resultSet.getRowCount(); index++) {
            rows.add(Map.of(
                    "id", resultSet.getString(index, 0),
                    "price", resultSet.getDouble(index, 1),
                    "ts", resultSet.getString(index, 2),
                    "timeInStatus", resultSet.getDouble(index, 3)
            ));
        }

        return Response.ok(rows).build();
    }
```

We can use this endpoint to return orders in a specific status that might be stuck. For example, the following command finds orders that have been in the `BEING_PREPARED` state for 30 seconds or more:

```
status="BEING_PREPARED"
millis="30000"
curl http://localhost:8080/orders/${status}/${millis} 2>/dev/null | jq '.[]'
```

The results of this command are shown in Example 9-9.

Example 9-9. Orders that might be stuck

```
{
"ts": "2022-12-12 13:48:11.129",
"price": 5596,
"id": "d5d34eaa-34be-4e60-97d6-9f420a4a7b8f",
"timeInStatus": 30.61
}
{
"ts": "2022-12-12 13:48:11.427",
"price": 5625,
"id": "a07eeb45-1120-44d6-9ab8-de8bcc6cc383",
"timeInStatus": 30.312
}
{
"ts": "2022-12-12 13:48:11.878",
"price": 8831,
"id": "4ce5a459-85dc-4868-810a-6b2c651ade7e",
"timeInStatus": 29.861
}
```

The following code renders this data in the dashboard for orders that have taken more than 60 seconds in the BEING_COOKED status:

```
st.subheader("Orders delayed while cooking")

popular_items = requests.get(
  f"{delivery_service_api}/orders/stuck/BEING_COOKED/60000").json()
df = pd.DataFrame(popular_items)[[
    "id", "price", "ts", "timeInStatus"
]].head(5)

html = convert_df(df)
st.markdown(html, unsafe_allow_html=True)
```

We can see a screenshot in Figure 9-7.

Orders delayed while cooking

id	price	ts	timeInStatus
b0c3d26b-b064-480f-9c4e-7da8784b0ea6	3790.0	2022-12-12 14:12:02.511	65.020
cd73a2ed-4a55-406b-af71-115dd480703c	10216.0	2022-12-12 14:12:03.451	64.080
454ed666-62a6-40f6-be35-399c3b6956b4	15361.0	2022-12-12 14:12:03.827	63.704
a1eeaaae-1784-47c0-aebf-df9ca2bf62e5	9210.0	2022-12-12 14:12:05.928	61.603
915ef1c9-75a8-4676-8e00-a716c098b4b6	6421.0	2022-12-12 14:12:06.931	60.600

Figure 9-7. Orders stuck while cooking

Our operators would then want to keep an eye on these orders to make sure they don't take too much longer and perhaps they could contact the kitchen to figure out what's going on if they do take longer.

Summary

In this chapter, we introduced Kafka Streams for order status, before ingesting that data into Apache Pinot. We used Pinot's upsert functionality to handle multiple order statuses, before updating the dashboard to highlight problematic orders. In the next chapter, we're going to add geospatial functionality to our application for delivery statuses.

CHAPTER 10

Geospatial Querying

AATD's users were very pleased with the publishing of an order's status in the pizza shop app. It's allowed them to see that their order is making progress and has also given them some indication of when it's likely to be delivered. But now that they've had a taste of real-time data, they want more!

The customer success team has received multiple requests for the pizza shop app to include a delivery tracker that shows where an order is once it leaves AATD's kitchen. In addition, AATD's operations team would like to be able to locate delivery vehicles. On multiple occasions, deliveries have been delayed due to traffic problems, and they'd like to be able to identify which vehicles are affected so that they can notify customers of a potential delay.

To add this functionality, we'll need to update the orders service to publish locations to a new `deliveryStatuses` stream. That stream will then be consumed by Apache Pinot, and we'll update the /orders/*<order_id>* endpoint to include the latest location. We will also go back and include the delivery latitude and longitude coordinates in the `orders` stream and add columns for those values to the equivalent table in Apache Pinot.

The traffic problems feature will also use the `deliveryStatuses` stream, but we'll add a new /orders/delayed/*<area>* endpoint to identify affected vehicles. This endpoint will be consumed by a new section of the dashboard.

Figure 10-1 shows the new pieces of infrastructure.

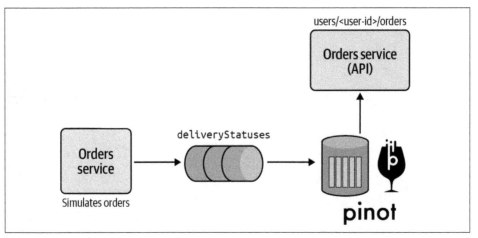

Figure 10-1. Delivery statuses architecture

Delivery Statuses

The GitHub repository includes a delivery status, which you can find in the *delivery-service* directory:

```
ls -lh delivery-service |
awk '{printf "%-4s %-2s %-2s %-5s %s\n", $5,$6,$7,$8,$9}'
```

This directory contains three files, as shown in Example 10-1.

Example 10-1. File listing of the delivery-service directory

```
307B 2  Nov 15:23 Dockerfile
5.0K 2  Nov 16:19 app.py
148B 2  Nov 15:55 requirements.txt
```

The *app.py* file contains an application that consumes messages from the `orders` stream and generates delivery statuses that are published to the `deliveryStatuses` topic using the Faust framework (*https://oreil.ly/4hkdU*). Faust is a stream processing library written by the engineering team at Robinhood and has been used to process billions of events every day as part of real-time data pipelines. It ports the ideas from Kafka Streams to Python and provides both stream processing and event processing.

We can see an example of the messages in the `deliveryStatuses` topic by running the following, which shows the delivery statuses for the order with ID `5e81f913-a7c9-48a4-afdc-51e08ee465e0`:

```
kcat -C -b localhost:29092 -t deliveryStatuses |
jq -c 'select(.id == "5e81f913-a7c9-48a4-afdc-51e08ee465e0")'
```

The results are shown in Example 10-2.

Example 10-2. Delivery locations as an order is on its way to the customer

```
{"id":"5e81f913-a7c9-48a4-afdc-51e08ee465e0","updatedAt":
"2022-10-25T15:55:06.477113",
"deliveryLat":"12.978268132410502","deliveryLon":"77.59408889388118",
"status": "IN_TRANSIT"}
{"id":"5e81f913-a7c9-48a4-afdc-51e08ee465e0","updatedAt":
"2022-10-25T15:55:11.477113",
"deliveryLat":"12.98006314499387","deliveryLon":"77.59363625531113",
"status": "IN_TRANSIT"}
{"id":"5e81f913-a7c9-48a4-afdc-51e08ee465e0","updatedAt":
"2022-10-25T15:55:16.477113",
"deliveryLat":"12.981858028693885","deliveryLon":"77.59318360492333",
"status": "IN_TRANSIT"}
{"id":"5e81f913-a7c9-48a4-afdc-51e08ee465e0","updatedAt":
"2022-10-25T15:55:21.477113",
"deliveryLat":"12.983652783521276","deliveryLon":"77.59273094271904",
"status": "IN_TRANSIT"}
{"id":"5e81f913-a7c9-48a4-afdc-51e08ee465e0","updatedAt":
"2022-10-25T15:55:26.477113",
"deliveryLat":"12.985447409486811","deliveryLon":"77.5922782686996",
"status": "IN_TRANSIT"}
```

We've also updated the orders service to store a delivery location (in latitude and longitude coordinates) for each user in MySQL. We can see the updated data by running the following query on our MySQL container:

```
SELECT id, first_name, last_name, email, lat, long
FROM pizzashop.users
LIMIT 5;
```

The results of running this query are shown in Table 10-1.

Table 10-1. Delivery latitude and longitude for first five users

id	first_name	last_name	email	lat	lon
1	Waldo	Morteo	wmorteo0@toplist.cz	13.00730910	77.69902478
2	Anselm	Tabbernor	atabbernor1@biglobe.ne.jp	13.05401507	77.54924136
3	Jane	Razoux	jrazoux2@webnode.com	12.97900746	77.68702230
4	Xavier	Adamski	xadamski3@free.fr	13.08019807	77.57086161
5	Adan	Griffith	agriffith4@rambler.ru	13.03410343	77.50085457

We're also now publishing latitude and longitude values to the orders stream, and we can see the updated messages in the orders stream by running the following:

```
kcat -C -b localhost:29092 -t orders | jq -c '{id, deliveryLat, deliveryLon}'
```

The results are shown in Example 10-3.

Example 10-3. Orders stream with latitudes and longitudes

```
{"id":"492651a0-8937-4e3d-93c3-38c8a521b28d","deliveryLat":"13.00730910",
"deliveryLon":"77.69902478"}
{"id":"5c9b8060-7003-4569-84a3-ea40c1eeeff4","deliveryLat":"13.05401507",
"deliveryLon":"77.54924136"}
{"id":"4b5f2f6c-f6ef-45e3-a623-a4ffc8c71421","deliveryLat":"12.97900746",
"deliveryLon":"77.68702230"}
{"id":"1a4d0bf5-d7c7-43c9-83cb-5d6cf10ce8a6","deliveryLat":"13.08019807",
"deliveryLon":"77.57086161"}
{"id":"12f131e9-35df-41cd-a88a-b461fa741745","deliveryLat":"13.03410343",
"deliveryLon":"77.50085457"}
```

Updating Apache Pinot

We need to make a couple of updates to Pinot as a result of adding delivery locations.

Orders

First, we need to update the `orders` table to include the delivery latitude and longitude for each order. A new schema that includes both of these fields is shown in Example 10-4.

Example 10-4. pinot/config/orders/schema-destination.json

```
{
  "schemaName": "orders",
  "dimensionFieldSpecs": [
    {"name": "id", "dataType": "STRING"},
    {"name": "userId", "dataType": "INT"},
    {"name": "deliveryLat", "dataType": "DOUBLE"},
    {"name": "deliveryLon", "dataType": "DOUBLE"},
    {"name": "items", "dataType": "JSON"}
  ],
  "metricFieldSpecs": [
    {"name": "productsOrdered", "dataType": "INT"},
    {"name": "totalQuantity", "dataType": "INT"},
    {"name": "price", "dataType": "DOUBLE"}
  ],
  "dateTimeFieldSpecs": [
    {
      "name": "ts",
      "dataType": "TIMESTAMP",
      "format": "1:MILLISECONDS:EPOCH",
      "granularity": "1:MILLISECONDS"
    }
```

```
    ]
}
```

We can update Pinot to include these fields by running the following command:

```
docker run -v $PWD/pinot/config:/config \
  --network rta \
  apachepinot/pinot:0.12.0 \
  AddSchema -schemaFile /config/orders/schema.json \
  -controllerHost pinot-controller \
  -exec
```

Let's now check that those fields have been hydrated by querying the table via the Pinot Data Explorer:

```
select id, deliveryLat, deliveryLon
from orders
limit 10
```

You should see something like the output in Table 10-2.

Table 10-2. Querying the orders table after delivery latitude/longitude have been added

deliveryLat	deliveryLon	id	location	ts
12.91634591	77.51759471	82dc37b2-4645-490e-8d1b-c366afad0ef6	8040536120459002164029d52b4a868bf6	2023-01-30 21:50:34.858
12.90113961	77.6770448	a62a4b6f-1e09-4443-ab4c-c4c55347dff8	8040536b54b3b67b524029cd622bc4290f	2023-01-30 21:50:35.031
13.01092717	77.48339447	c99759e7-fce8-4478-a934-c0a903083cba	8040535eefef5bede7402a05983efb935f	2023-01-30 21:50:35.057
13.04882104	77.5031806	5831a5e6-7d1f-4f0b-b0c4-f6ef5b781895	80405360341c673ed3402a18ff1244503c	2023-01-30 21:50:35.238
12.91142212	77.68324356	8292819a-01c1-4afe-8f1b-540d314066bc	8040536bba433259c44029d2a5eb8c8081	2023-01-30 21:50:35.491
13.0932961	77.60812634	48851f6f-3003-473c-a2df-72e21ea071bf	80405366eb8abd88b7402a2fc481a4b04e	2023-01-30 21:50:35.712
12.88820332	77.63336297	1e0b6fca-0fe5-4561-b4c2-f69e2eeea169	804053688904d6a96f4029c6c295e7327f	2023-01-30 21:50:35.73
13.09098746	77.60308604	b4472d4d-f98e-427a-8663-fd3842256d37	8040536698f6309e58402a2e95e88a179b	2023-01-30 21:50:36.283
12.99484932	77.48369871	0fb52e16-958f-4742-b667-2392379c5675	8040535ef4eb6f24504029fd5ce3dbb218	2023-01-30 21:50:36.345
12.89129797	77.53741272	b6fe2af0-2040-4f9c-a5ae-2e9d63bc6c88	8040536264f85236af4029c8583520484a	2023-01-30 21:50:36.451

The deliveryLat and deliveryLon fields will only be available on newly ingested data. Records that have already been ingested will have a null value for these fields.

Delivery Statuses

Since we're only interested in the latest delivery location, we're going to create a Pinot upserts table again, similar to the orders_enriched table. Let's start with the schema, which is shown in Example 10-5.

Example 10-5. pinot/config/deliveryStatuses/schema.json

```
{
    "schemaName": "deliveryStatuses",
    "primaryKeyColumns": ["id"],
    "dimensionFieldSpecs": [
      {"name": "id", "dataType": "STRING"},
      {"name": "deliveryLat", "dataType": "DOUBLE"},
      {"name": "deliveryLon", "dataType": "DOUBLE"},
      {"name": "status", "dataType": "STRING"},
      {"name": "location", "dataType": "BYTES"}
    ],
    "dateTimeFieldSpecs": [
      {
        "name": "ts",
        "dataType": "TIMESTAMP",
        "format": "1:MILLISECONDS:EPOCH",
        "granularity": "1:MILLISECONDS"
      }
    ]
  }
```

The id, deliveryLat, and deliveryLon fields are mapped directly from the data source. location is going to represent a geospatial point, which will be hydrated by a transformation function.

The table config is shown in Example 10-6.

Example 10-6. pinot/config/deliveryStatuses/table.json

```
{
    "tableName": "deliveryStatuses",
    "tableType": "REALTIME",
    "segmentsConfig": {
      "timeColumnName": "ts",
      "timeType": "MILLISECONDS",
      "retentionTimeUnit": "DAYS",
```

```
    "retentionTimeValue": "1",
    "schemaName": "deliveryStatuses",
    "replicasPerPartition": "1"
},
"tenants": {},
"upsertConfig": {"mode": "FULL"},
"fieldConfigList": [
  {
    "name": "location",
    "encodingType":"RAW",
    "indexType":"H3",
    "properties": {"resolutions": "5"}
  }
],
"tableIndexConfig": {
  "loadMode": "MMAP",
  "streamConfigs": {
    "streamType": "kafka",
    "stream.kafka.consumer.type": "lowLevel",
    "stream.kafka.topic.name": "deliveryStatuses",
    "stream.kafka.decoder.class.name":
      "org.apache.pinot.plugin.stream.kafka.KafkaJSONMessageDecoder",
    "stream.kafka.consumer.factory.class.name":
      "org.apache.pinot.plugin.stream.kafka20.KafkaConsumerFactory",
    "stream.kafka.broker.list": "kafka:9092",
    "stream.kafka.consumer.prop.auto.offset.reset": "smallest"
  }
},
"ingestionConfig": {
  "transformConfigs": [
    {
      "columnName": "ts",
      "transformFunction":
      "FromDateTime(\"updatedAt\", 'yyyy-MM-dd''T''HH:mm:ss.SSSSSS')"
    },
    {
      "columnName": "location",
      "transformFunction": "stPoint(deliveryLon,deliveryLat, 1)"
    }
  ]
},
"metadata": {"customConfigs": {}},
"routing": {"instanceSelectorType": "strictReplicaGroup"}
}
```

The transformation function uses the stPoint function, which has the following sig-
nature: STPOINT(x, y, isGeography). This function returns a geography point
object with the provided coordinate values.

The location column also has a geospatial index, defined by the JSON in
Example 10-7.

Example 10-7. Geospatial index config for `deliveryStatuses` table

```
"fieldConfigList": [
  {
    "name": "location",
    "encodingType":"RAW",
    "indexType":"H3",
    "properties": {"resolutions": "5"}
  }
],
```

Geospatial indexing enables efficient querying of location-based data, such as latitude and longitude coordinates or geographical shapes. Apache Pinot's geospatial index is based on Uber's Hexagonal Hierarchical Spatial Index (H3) library (*https://oreil.ly/ NFU_Z*).

This library provides hexagon-based hierarchical gridding. Indexing a point means that the point is translated to a geoId, which corresponds to a hexagon. Its neighbors in H3 can be approximated by a ring of hexagons. Direct neighbors have a distance of 1, their neighbors are at a distance of 2, and so on.

For example, in Figure 10-2, the central hexagon covers the center of Bengaluru, with different colors for neighbors at distance 1, at distance 2, and at distance 3.

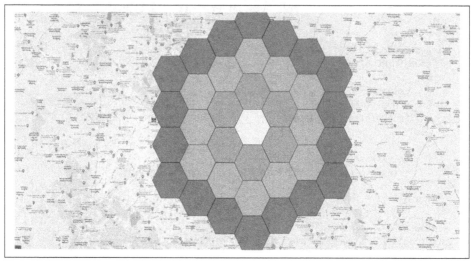

Figure 10-2. H3 hexagons overlaid on Bengaluru

The query engine makes use of these hexagons when finding points that exist within a given a radius of a point or those points that are inside or outside a polygon area.

We'll create this table and schema by running the following:

```
docker run -v $PWD/pinot/config:/config \
  --network rta \
  apachepinot/pinot:0.12.0-arm64 \
  AddTable -schemaFile /config/deliveryStatuses/schema.json \
          -tableConfigFile /config/deliveryStatuses/table.json \
          -controllerHost pinot-controller \
          -exec
```

Once that table is created, we can go to the Pinot Data Explorer and check that the table is being populated by writing the following query:

```
select *
from deliveryStatuses
limit 10
```

The results of running this query can be seen in Table 10-3.

Table 10-3. Querying deliveryStatuses table

deliveryLat	deliveryLon	id	ts
12.977514	77.59513559	816b9d84-9426-4055-9d48-54d11496bfbe	2022-12-08 12:03:50.386
12.9769286	77.59181282	d06545bb-48ef-4e0a-8d7f-e2916cef2508	2022-12-08 12:03:51.7
12.99280883	77.58791287	a14ff1d9-59d7-456e-a205-37faf274145d	2022-12-08 12:03:55.573
12.96761213	77.57942433	de283949-76a3-4898-ac3e-0bd8bc9ab0bc	2022-12-08 12:04:04.511
12.98316363	77.59789082	08309572-4b20-42a6-8cc7-340b42f636ae	2022-12-08 12:04:10.787
12.97462394	77.60476875	f45eb73f-c38d-4176-9233-54bb62ec2716	2022-12-08 12:04:11.762
12.977514	77.59513559	d8bb71a6-e23e-483e-9687-6c7da0da2a62	2022-12-08 12:04:13.729
12.97580839	77.59262398	2d115b4d-efe6-4988-a04b-fe78e3536ff9	2022-12-08 12:04:15.715
12.97786261	77.59274363	3931d15b-f99a-43ea-8d62-5fcaceba64b5	2022-12-08 12:04:20.994
12.96716917	77.57689339	3d1036f4-f7ba-41ef-aef8-07f47b4df6a7	2022-12-08 12:04:23.29

We can also zoom in on one of those orders and return all the delivery locations over time:

```
select deliveryLat, deliveryLon, id, ts
from deliveryStatuses
WHERE id = '816b9d84-9426-4055-9d48-54d11496bfbe'
limit 10
option(skipUpsert=true)
```

The results of running this query can be seen in Table 10-4.

Table 10-4. Querying `deliveryStatuses` for order 816b9d84-9426-4055-9d48-54d11496bfbe

deliveryLat	deliveryLon	id	ts
12.978268132410502	77.59408889388118	816b9d84-9426-4055-9d48-54d11496bfbe	2022-12-08 12:03:46.386
12.97807961104748	77.59435056811378	816b9d84-9426-4055-9d48-54d11496bfbe	2022-12-08 12:03:47.386
12.977891081858383	77.59461224221113	816b9d84-9426-4055-9d48-54d11496bfbe	2022-12-08 12:03:48.386
12.97770254484272	77.5948739161732	816b9d84-9426-4055-9d48-54d11496bfbe	2022-12-08 12:03:49.386
12.977514	77.59513559	816b9d84-9426-4055-9d48-54d11496bfbe	2022-12-08 12:03:50.386

We can also run a query to see how many deliveries are within a particular virtual perimeter around a real area, known as a *geofence*. Perhaps the operations team has information that there's been an accident in a certain part of the city and wants to see how many drivers are potentially stuck. An example query is shown here:

```
select count(*)
from deliveryStatuses
WHERE ST_Contains(
        ST_GeomFromText('POLYGON((
            77.6110752789269 12.967434625129457,
            77.61949358844464 12.972227849153782,
            77.62067778131079 12.966846580403327,
            77.61861133323839 12.96537193573893,
            77.61507457042217 12.965872682158846,
            77.6110752789269 12.967434625129457))'),
        toGeometry(location)
    ) = 1
AND status = 'IN_TRANSIT'
```

This query uses the `ST_Contains` function, which is defined in its documentation (*https://oreil.ly/5K4L5*) as follows:

> Returns true if and only if no points of the second geometry/geography lie in the exterior of the first geometry/geography, and at least one point of the interior of the first geometry lies in the interior of the second geometry.

This doesn't make any mention of the geospatial index that we defined earlier, so how does that come into play? Let's imagine that the preceding query is trying to find the drivers that are currently located inside the white outline shown in Figure 10-3.

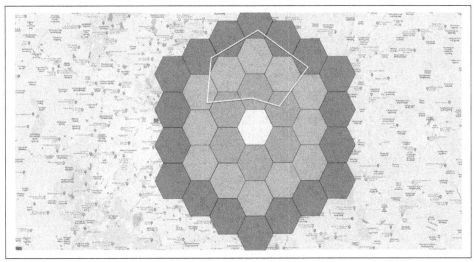

Figure 10-3. A polygon on top of H3 hexagons overlaid on Bengaluru

Pinot's query planner will first find all the coordinates on the exterior of the polygon. It will then find the hexagons that fit within that geofence. Those hexagons get added to the potential cells list.

The query planner then takes each of those hexagons and checks whether they fit completely inside the original polygon. If they do, then they get added to the fully contained cells list. If we have any cells in both lists, we remove them from the potential cells list.

Next, we find the records for the fully contained cells list and those for the potential cells list. We then return those in the fully contained list and apply the ST_Contains predicate to the potential list to work out which records should be returned.

The results of running this query can be seen in Table 10-5.

Table 10-5. Checking how many deliveries are stuck

count(*)
30

Let's have a look at some of the stuck deliveries:

```
select ts, id, deliveryLat, deliveryLon
from deliveryStatuses
WHERE ST_Contains(
        ST_GeomFromText('POLYGON((
            77.6110752789269 12.967434625129457,
            77.61949358844464 12.972227849153782,
            77.62067778131079 12.966846580403327,
            77.61861133323839 12.96537193573893,
            77.61507457042217 12.965872682158846,
            77.6110752789269 12.967434625129457))'),
        toGeometry(location)
    ) = 1
AND status = 'IN_TRANSIT'
LIMIT 10
```

The results of running this query can be seen in Table 10-6.

Table 10-6. Deliveries that are stuck

ts	id	deliveryLat	deliveryLon
2023-01-31 03:47:01.813	4d0f35e4-c5a1-4fed-a8ae-0206fa4f652a	12.96956644	77.62002299
2023-01-31 04:03:12.78	36767ba0-997c-409d-9e6d-abb4e04a82f4	12.9689433	77.61624128
2023-01-31 04:21:46.351	0f532b85-bc35-4c1b-8079-b96d6082fd83	12.96750099	77.61282588
2023-01-31 04:22:40.528	b8f8b8b3-8b7b-4085-bf17-eb70c031f2c7	12.96956644	77.62002299
2023-01-31 04:38:42.43	9cf65d90-d1dc-4ecc-9ec7-e838769e45ab	12.96853289	77.61506311
2023-01-31 04:57:06.506	1003fd38-9815-47e9-af44-415eacde0738	12.96886296	77.61940757
2023-01-31 05:14:40.412	9951a303-5eec-420d-bec8-c9c1036cfeb1	12.9693779	77.6188917
2023-01-31 05:54:38.991	cfbd8a1a-1ab8-43f7-b111-50a71f89177a	12.96853289	77.61506311
2023-01-31 06:03:39.624	51bc79b0-1af1-42c3-98b0-34ad52256140	12.96956644	77.62002299
2023-01-31 06:04:02.374	aca66367-4364-48eb-8682-b7b21e4aaf14	12.9693779	77.6188917

Updating the Orders Service

Next, we're going to update the orders service to return this data.

Individual Orders

First, /orders/*<order-id>* will be updated to have the following structure:

```
[
    "user": {
        "deliveryLat": "<deliveryLat>",
        "deliveryLon": "<deliveryLon>",
        "id": "<userId>",
    },
    "statuses": [
```

```
        {"ts":"<ts1>","status":"<status1>"}
    ],
    "products": [
        {
            "image": "<image>",
            "price": "<price>",
            "product": "<product>",
            "quantity": "<quantity>"
        }
    ],
    "deliveryStatus": {
        "ts": "<timestamp>",
        "deliveryLat": "<latitudeOfDeliveryVehicle>",
        "deliveryLon": "<longitudeOfDeliveryVehicle>"
    }
]
```

We won't reproduce the whole order function, but we'll make an update to the orders query, as well as adding a new query to retrieve the delivery status:

```
@GET
@Path("/{orderId}")
public Response order(@PathParam("orderId") String orderId) {
  // Get the userId and delivery location
  String userQuery = DSL.using(SQLDialect.POSTGRES)
        .select(field("userId"))
        .select(field("deliveryLat"))
        .select(field("deliveryLon"))
        .from("orders")
        .where(field("id").eq(field("'" + orderId + "'")))
        .getSQL();
  ResultSet userResultSet = runQuery(connection, userQuery);
  Stream<Map<String, Object>> userInfo = IntStream.range(0,
                userResultSet.getRowCount())
        .mapToObj(index -> Map.of(
                "id", userResultSet.getString(index, 0),
                "deliveryLat", userResultSet.getDouble(index, 1),
                "deliveryLon", userResultSet.getDouble(index, 2)
        ));

  // ...

  // Get the current location of the delivery
  String deliveryStatusQuery = DSL.using(SQLDialect.POSTGRES)
        .select(
                field("ToDateTime(ts, 'YYYY-MM-dd HH:mm:ss')").as("ts"),
                field("deliveryLat"),
                field("deliveryLon")
        )
        .from("deliveryStatuses")
        .where(field("id").eq(field("'" + orderId + "'")))
        .getSQL();
  ResultSet deliveryStatusResultSet = runQuery(connection, deliveryStatusQuery);
```

```
Stream<Map<String, Object>> deliveryStatus = IntStream.range(0,
                deliveryStatusResultSet.getRowCount())
        .mapToObj(index -> Map.of(
                "timestamp", deliveryStatusResultSet.getString(index, 0),
                "lat", deliveryStatusResultSet.getDouble(index, 1),
                "lon", deliveryStatusResultSet.getDouble(index, 2)
        ));

    Map<String, Object> response = new HashMap<>(Map.of(
            "user", userInfo,
            "products", products,
            "statuses", statuses
    ));

    deliveryStatus.findFirst().ifPresent(stringObjectMap ->
            response.put("deliveryStatus", stringObjectMap));

    return Response.ok(response).build();
}
```

We can test it out by running the following command:

```
orderId="f16f61be-a082-478c-a781-39bc69d174dc"
curl http://localhost:8080/orders/${orderId} 2>/dev/null | jq '.'
```

The results of this command are shown in Example 10-8.

Example 10-8. The details for order f16f61be-a082-478c-a781-39bc69d174dc

```
{
  "user": {
    "deliveryLat": 12.98727479,
    "deliveryLon": 77.7178702,
    "id": 3765,
  },
  "deliveryStatus": {
    "lat": 12.979204959662848,
    "lon": 77.60707835711453,
    "timestamp": "2022-10-26 14:00:39"
  },
  "products": [
    {
      "image": "https://oreil.ly/vEv1e",
      "price": 175,
      "product": "Non Veg Loaded",
      "quantity": 2
    },
    {
      "image": "https://oreil.ly/ms7dp",
      "price": 385,
      "product": "Veggie Paradise",
      "quantity": 2
```

```
    }
  ],
  "statuses": [
    {"status": "OUT_FOR_DELIVERY", "timestamp": "2022-10-26 14:00:05"},
    {"status": "BEING_COOKED", "timestamp": "2022-10-26 13:59:16"},
    {"status": "BEING_PREPARED", "timestamp": "2022-10-26 13:59:02"},
    {"status": "ORDER_CONFIRMED", "timestamp": "2022-10-26 13:58:50"},
    {"status": "PLACED_ORDER", "timestamp": "2022-10-26 13:58:28"}
  ],
}
```

Delayed Orders by Area

We're also going to add a new endpoint, /orders/<order-id>, which will return any of the deliveries that are within a provided polygon. This endpoint will have the following structure:

```
[
    {
        "deliveryLat": "<deliveryLat>",
        "deliveryLon": "<deliveryLon>",
        "id": "<id>>",
        "ts": "<ts>"
    }
]
```

We'll add the following code to OrdersResource:

```java
@GET
@Path("/delayed/{area}")
public Response Delayed(@PathParam("area") String area) {
    String query = DSL.using(SQLDialect.POSTGRES)
            .select(
                    field("ts"),
                    field("id"),
                    field("deliveryLat"),
                    field("deliveryLon")
            )
            .from("deliveryStatuses")
            .where(field("status").eq(field("'" + "IN_TRANSIT" + "'")))
            .and(field("ST_Contains(ST_GeomFromText('" + area + "'),
                            toGeometry(location)) = 1")
                        .coerce(Boolean.class))
            .orderBy(field("ts"))
            .getSQL();

    ResultSet resultSet = runQuery(connection, query);

    List<Map<String, Object>> rows = new ArrayList<>();
    for (int index = 0; index < resultSet.getRowCount(); index++) {
        rows.add(Map.of(
                "ts", resultSet.getString(index, 0),
```

```
            "id", resultSet.getString(index, 1),
            "deliveryLat", resultSet.getDouble(index, 2),
            "deliveryLon", resultSet.getDouble(index, 3)
        ));
    }

    return Response.ok(rows).build();
}
```

We can test it out by running the following command:

```
area=$(cat <<-END
POLYGON((
77.6110752789269 12.967434625129457,
77.61949358844464 12.972227849153782,
77.62067778131079 12.966846580403327,
77.61861133323839 12.96537193573893,
77.61507457042217 12.965872682158846,
77.6110752789269 12.967434625129457))
END
)

curl "http://localhost:8082/orders/delayed/$(echo ${area} | jq -sRr @uri)" \
  2>/dev/null | jq -c '.[]'
```

The results of this command are shown in Example 10-9.

Example 10-9. Orders that are within a polygon

```
{"deliveryLat":12.968781979860712,"id":"49a847ce-7be4-4b7b-a476-418f3fe9ade8",
"deliveryLon":77.61996813820166,"ts":"2023-01-31 10:51:09.423"}
{"deliveryLat":12.966912327254263,"id":"2b49522b-8367-42b7-b953-6182d392f5a8",
"deliveryLon":77.61996881341163,"ts":"2023-01-31 10:51:09.855"}
{"deliveryLat":12.968905738349724,"id":"2592737e-85f6-4c9c-9d26-6512e0a79e1b",
"deliveryLon":77.61618795631033,"ts":"2023-01-31 10:51:10.007"}
{"deliveryLat":12.966653982500155,"id":"2fdeb13f-c36d-4513-8e2f-7874e91cb26b",
"deliveryLon":77.61735699385572,"ts":"2023-01-31 10:59:35.629"}
{"deliveryLat":12.96737038553749,"id":"808d78f6-9343-4d21-adc4-c2f707a9fd24",
"deliveryLon":77.61805308090885,"ts":"2023-01-31 10:59:35.761"}
```

Consuming the New API Endpoints

We can then wire things up on the frontend and create a map that's updated every second with the latest delivery location. A screenshot from this map is shown in Figure 10-4.

Figure 10-4. A pizza en route to its delivery location

We can also add the following code to the dashboard to show the deliveries that might be stuck:

```python
import urllib.parse

area = """
POLYGON((
    77.6110752789269 12.967434625129457,
    77.61949358844464 12.972227849153782,
    77.62067778131079 12.966846580403327,
    77.61861133323839 12.96537193573893,
    77.61507457042217 12.965872682158846,
    77.6110752789269 12.967434625129457
))
"""
encoded_area = urllib.parse.quote(area)
delayed_orders = requests.get(
                f"{delivery_service_api}/orders/delayed/{encoded_area}").json()
st.subheader("Orders stuck in transit")

df = pd.DataFrame(delayed_orders)[[
    "id", "ts", "deliveryLat", "deliveryLon"
```

```
]].head(5)

html = convert_df(df)
st.markdown(html, unsafe_allow_html=True)
```

A screenshot from this part of the dashboard is shown in Figure 10-5.

Orders stuck in transit			
id	ts	deliveryLat	deliveryLon
49a847ce-7be4-4b7b-a476-418f3fe9ade8	2023-01-31 10:51:09.423	12.968782	77.619968
2b49522b-8367-42b7-b953-6182d392f5a8	2023-01-31 10:51:09.855	12.966912	77.619969
2592737e-85f6-4c9c-9d26-6512e0a79e1b	2023-01-31 10:51:10.007	12.968906	77.616188
2fdeb13f-c36d-4513-8e2f-7874e91cb26b	2023-01-31 10:59:35.629	12.966654	77.617357
808d78f6-9343-4d21-adc4-c2f707a9fd24	2023-01-31 10:59:35.761	12.967370	77.618053

Figure 10-5. Orders that are potentially stuck

Summary

This was the final hands-on chapter in the book! In this chapter, we introduced Kafka Streams for order and delivery status, before ingesting that data into Apache Pinot. We used Pinot's upsert functionality to handle the multiple order and delivery statuses before updating the dashboard to highlight problematic orders. In the next chapter, we're going to look at production considerations for real-time analytics applications.

CHAPTER 11

Production Considerations

We have the pizza shop application working on our machine, but it's no good running there because only we can use it; now we need to get it into production. In this chapter, we'll be covering some of the things to keep in mind when moving a real-time analytics application from your local machine into production.

When moving into production, we're optimizing for performance, reliability, and cost. This isn't the most exciting chapter, but the information included here will hopefully be useful for helping you run your applications in a live environment.

Before we get into the nitty-gritty, let's remind ourselves about the high-level design of a real-time analytics system, as shown in Figure 11-1.

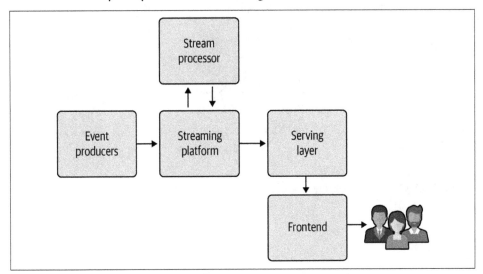

Figure 11-1. Real-time analytics stack

Preproduction

Before going into production, we need to design our production architecture, which includes capacity planning and choosing our deployment platform.

Capacity Planning

Capacity planning is the process of determining the amount of required resources, mostly in terms of computing power and storage. This isn't a one-time task, but rather a continuous process that requires regular monitoring and adjustment to adapt to changing demands and requirements.

We'll have to collaborate with a variety of stakeholders, including operations and business users, to understand their needs and goals. Figure 11-2 shows the cycle of capacity planning.

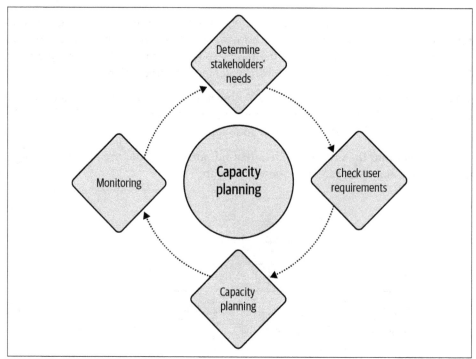

Figure 11-2. Capacity planning workflow

We'll need to predict both the current and future needs for our application and work out the resources we'll need. It is an important undertaking, as it will help ensure that the architecture can handle expected load as well as allow for future growth.

It will involve working out a partitioning strategy, expected throughput, data retention policy, total data size, as well as the data granularity that we want in different parts of the system. Let's start with data partitioning.

Data Partitioning

The data stored in topics in streaming data platforms is split into partitions. An individual topic, therefore, contains but a fraction of the data for that topic. While the topic is a logical concept, a *partition* is the smallest storage unit that holds a subset of records owned by a topic. Each partition is a single log file, where records are written in an append-only fashion.

Working out the number of partitions to use is an important early decision. When developing locally, we can probably get away with a single partition because we are dealing with much smaller throughput requirements than we'll have once the system is properly in use.

Partitions are the way that streaming data platforms achieve scalability. Each server (sometimes called a *broker*) holds a subset of the records that belong to the entire cluster. Partitions for a particular topic will be distributed across servers.

By spreading partitions across multiple brokers, a single topic can be scaled horizontally to provide performance far beyond a single server's ability. One part of the scaling is that we can write events at a high throughput, as shown in Figure 11-3.

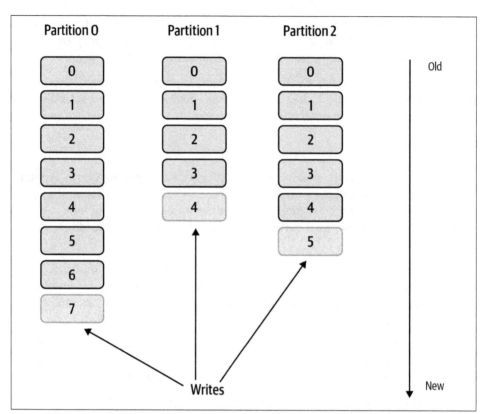

Figure 11-3. Multiple producers writing data

Those topics can also be consumed by multiple consumers in parallel. Having to serve all partitions from a single broker would severely limit the number of consumers that we could support. Partitions on multiple servers enable more consumers, which is vital, as it helps reduce the latency of data moving from the streaming data platform to the stream processor and serving layer. Each of these consumers will read data at different offsets, as shown in Figure 11-4.

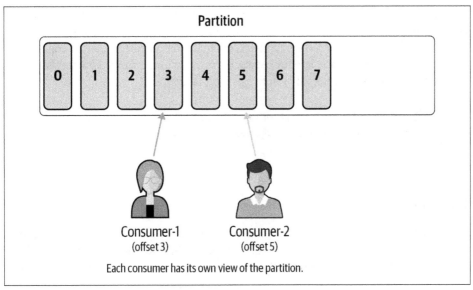

Figure 11-4. Multiple consumers reading data

Consumers will keep track of the last offset that's been read so that they can resume reading from the correct place in the event of a crash.

We now understand why having more than one partition is useful from the perspective of producing and consuming data, but how do we work out the number of partitions to use?

Jun Rao, a cofounder of Confluent (which provides the leading streaming platform based on Apache Kafka), gives us a useful formula for working out the number of partitions that we need (*https://oreil.ly/FDH80*). Here is the formula:

```
Number of partitions = max(
    target throughput / producer throughput,
    target throughput / consumer throughput
)
```

For example, if we have a target throughput of 10,000 messages per second with 3,000 messages per second by each producer and 5,000 messages per second consumed by each consumer, we'll fill in the values like this:

```
Number of partitions = max(10000 / 3000, 10000 / 5000)
Number of partitions = max(3.3, 2)
Number of partitions = 3
```

We can then adjust the number of partitions based on the size of each event, replication factor, type of acknowledgment, and so on.

The number of partitions will help determine the number of cores that we require in the serving layer component that's responsible for ingesting data. We want to have at least as many cores as we have partitions, so that each partition can be ingested in parallel. This will reduce the latency between the data being received by the streaming data platform and being queryable in the serving layer.

 The result from this formula should be used as a starting point, which may need to be adjusted as we run data through the system.

Throughput

We need to know both the expected read and write throughput in queries per second (QPS) at the serving layer so that we can work out the number of servers required. The QPS breaks down into read QPS and write QPS, which affect different parts of the architecture.

Although the various serving layers use different terminology, each will deploy servers with at least the following responsibilities:

Controller
  Manages cluster and partition assignment, while maintaining a mapping of segments to servers. Undertakes other management activities like segment retention and validation.

Server
  Stores the data and serves it to the broker to answer queries.

Broker
  Accepts queries from clients and forwards them to the right servers. Collects results from those servers and consolidates them into a response that's sent back to the client.

Figure 11-5 shows where the architecture will be impacted by the number of queries per second.

The *read QPS* helps determine the number of cores needed in the server and broker components. For a user-facing analytics use case, we would expect to have a read QPS in the hundreds or thousands or perhaps higher. For an internal dashboarding or reporting use case, we might see a read QPS in the lower double digits.

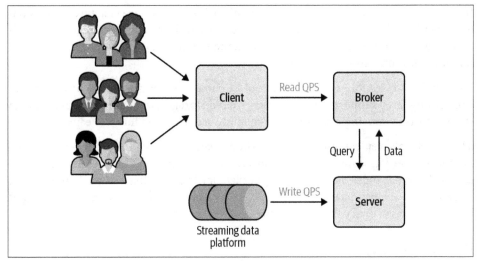

Figure 11-5. Read and write queries per second

The *write QPS* indicates the rate of ingestion in events per second. This is generally used in the context of data being ingested from a real-time streaming source. The write QPS primarily helps determine the number of cores needed in the server component to support real-time ingestion.

Data Retention

In the pizza shop example that we used throughout the book, we kept all the data around forever. In a production environment, we would need to have a data retention policy, as we don't have infinite storage space! This policy would be defined based on business and compliance requirements as well as data storage costs.

In a real-time analytics architecture, data is mostly stored in the streaming data platform and serving layer. The stream processor may also store copies of the data so that it can efficiently compute windowed aggregations and materialized views. We will focus on the streaming data platform and the serving layer, which will likely have separate data retention policies.

Event data would typically be retained in the streaming data platform for a few days, up to about a week. The actual retention period will be influenced by the volume of data that's being produced and the corresponding cost of storage.

If we need to retain data so that we can do historical analysis, we can always offload it to a data lake. In addition, we might also choose to keep the data around for a bit longer in the serving layer so that we can write queries that compare what's happening now with some time in the past.

We should also explore whether our tool of choice for the streaming data platform and serving layer supports tiered storage. Tiered storage can help reduce overall data storage costs by moving older or less frequently accessed data into a cheaper tier.

There are, however, trade-offs that we should keep in mind. At the streaming data platform, older log segments will be moved into cheaper storage, which means a consumer that reads older data will see higher latency in retrieving events. At the serving layer, queries against data stored in the cheaper storage will be slower, but that might be fine if we don't query that data often.

Data Granularity

Alongside data retention, we need to decide on the data granularity that we want to use in different parts of the stack. *Data granularity* refers to the level of detail of the events or records in different parts of the stack.

In the streaming data platform, we will have the raw events themselves, which give us the most fine-grained information.

When we're moving data into the serving layer, we might choose to aggregate the data if we know that we're never going to query it at the event level. For example, if a user visited a web page three times in a session, we might roll those page views up into one event that includes the page URL and a `"timesVisited": 3` property.

Once we've aggregated the data, it might not be possible to get it back in its original state, because it may have already been removed from an upstream system. The serving layer will often let you store data at an event level initially and then roll it up after a certain amount of time has passed, which might be an acceptable compromise.

Total Data Size

We need to know the total amount of data that we're planning to store so that we can work out the number of servers to provision. We can start by predicting the amount of data that's likely to be produced each day. If we multiply this value by the retention period, we'll have a rough idea of how much data we'll be dealing with at any one time.

We can then see whether we need to adjust the number of servers that we came up with after computing the read and write QPS.

Replication Factor

The *replication factor* determines how many copies of the data we hold and applies to both the streaming data platform and serving layer. We replicate the data so that we have resilience in our cluster in case servers go down.

We would typically set a replication factor of three, which means that we have three copies of each partition. Using Apache Kafka as an example of the streaming data platform and Apache Pinot as a serving layer, this means we would have multiple Kafka brokers and multiple Pinot server instances to handle the replication.

Deployment Platform

Now that we've thought about the required hardware, we need to consider where we're going to deploy our application. At a high level, we have the choice of deploying components to our own infrastructure or using a hosted (SaaS) service. Our decision will depend on several factors, which we'll consider in this section.

In-House Skills

The first thing to consider is the skills that we have in our team and organization. The tools that we've described in this book are complex distributed systems that require specialized skills and expertise to deploy and maintain.

If your team doesn't have the necessary skills and experience to set up and maintain this type of infrastructure, using a hosted offering might be more efficient and cost-effective, at least to start with. SaaS providers will handle the underlying infrastructure and maintenance, freeing up your team to focus on building real-time analytics applications.

On the other hand, if your team does have the necessary skills and experience, you may want to consider deploying in-house to have more control over the infrastructure and avoid potential limitations of a SaaS offering.

Data Privacy and Security

Data privacy and security are important to keep in mind. We can actually make arguments for and against SaaS in this regard.

If we use SaaS, our data is stored in the provider's infrastructure, which may raise privacy and security concerns. We may therefore need to run things by the regulatory and compliance team to make sure that they are happy with us storing our data elsewhere.

On the other hand, SaaS providers will likely have more experience at ensuring the security of this type of infrastructure, as well as the resources to manage security and compliance.

Some SaaS providers may also offer a service where they deploy part of their platform onto our infrastructure. They will typically have a control plane that manages the SaaS platform components in their own infrastructure, but will host the data plane inside our virtual private cloud. The SaaS platform provider will export system metrics and logs from our cluster so that it can monitor, detect, alert, and automatically handle any failures. This setup lets us keep control of our data, while still getting the benefits of a hosted service.

Regardless of our choice, we should establish clear privacy and security policies to make sure that our data is protected at all times.

Cost

Cost is a tricky one because what seems a better value in the short term might not be a better value in the long term. In addition to comparing the absolute cost, we should keep in mind that SaaS and in-house options have different cost structures.

Self-hosting may initially appear to be more cost-effective, but there may be hidden costs associated with managing and maintaining the infrastructure over time. We may have to pay for hardware and software licenses, ongoing maintenance and upgrades, as well as hire additional staff to manage the infrastructure.

SaaS services charge a premium, but this price includes maintenance, support, and upgrades. When using SaaS, we're also paying for the flexibility that it provides. We pay for the infrastructure only as we're using it. This makes it a good choice if we want to stand up infrastructure for experiments or short-term projects.

We therefore need to evaluate the total cost of ownership of both of these options over time. That analysis should include the opportunity costs associated with managing infrastructure rather than focusing on core business activities.

Control

If we opt to go with a SaaS solution, we will have less control over our deployment and may not be able to configure it exactly as we want. Perhaps we won't be able to use a specific plug-in that we want to use because the provider doesn't support it. Or maybe we won't be able to extract all the metrics that we want to track the health of our estate.

Overall, each deployment option has pros and cons, but a useful rule of thumb is that if you have a small or new team, start with a SaaS platform and go from there.

Postproduction

We've now deployed our application to production, and we need to keep an eye on it to make sure it's performing as expected. We also want to make sure that our data quality stays high.

Monitoring and Alerting

Monitoring and alerting are critical for ensuring the health and performance of the components in the real-time analytics stack. By monitoring key metrics and setting up alerts, we can proactively identify and rectify issues before they get out of control.

The amount and type of monitoring required depends to some extent on our deployment choice. If we're using a SaaS offering, the provider will be tracking the uptime of components to ensure that our service-level agreement (SLA) is met. If not, we'll need to monitor everything ourselves.

But, regardless of deployment choice, we'll still want to monitor some things ourselves. The actual names of metrics will vary depending on the product, but we should keep an eye on the next two points.

Streaming data platform

Network request rate
> What is the network traffic for each broker? When a broker's bandwidth goes above a certain threshold, it might indicate that we need to scale up the number of brokers.

Requests per second
> How many requests are being received by producers and consumers?

Request failure rate
> How many requests are failing, especially with respect to the producer?

Serving layer

Ingestion lag
> How far behind the streaming data platform is the serving layer with respect to the last offset ingested?

Consumption exceptions
> How many errors did we encounter when ingesting data?

Query latency
> How long is it taking to serve the results of a query to the user?

We'll then need to decide which tool we're going to use to track these metrics.

Lots of options are available, including Prometheus and Graphite, if you want to host it yourself. If you prefer to use a cloud-based monitoring platform, New Relic and Datadog are popular choices. And if you want fine-grained querying capabilities, you might even choose to use a time-series database like InfluxDB.

Data Governance

Data governance is perhaps not the most exciting topic, but it is something to think about when moving a real-time analytics app into production. We want to ensure that the right data is being streamed into Kafka and then downstream, and, if it isn't, we need to know about it. We'll also want to think about data access control and security.

Kafka's solution to data governance is a schema registry, which is an application that lives outside the Kafka cluster and handles the distribution of schemas to the producers and consumers.

The producer will use the schema to serialize events sent to Kafka, and the consumer will use the schema to deserialize them. The producer API will make sure that incompatible messages can't be produced, and the consumer API will prevent incompatible messages from being consumed. You can see how this works in Figure 11-6.

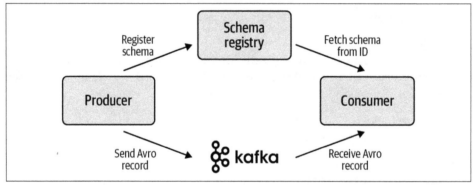

Figure 11-6. Schema registry

Many data formats let you define schemas, but the most popular one in the real-time analytics ecosystem is Avro, an open source data-serialization system that provides compact, fast, and efficient binary data encoding that can be used across multiple programming languages.

Confluent Schema Registry is the most popular registry, but it works only with Kafka. Redpanda and Pulsar also have their own registries. These schema registries usually have support for evolving the schema over time.

The components in the real-time analytics stack all have support for access control, which we'll want to enable when we put our application into a production environment.

Summary

In this chapter, we've covered some of the decisions that you'll have to make when taking a real-time analytics application from your machine to a production environment. We did some capacity planning, chose a deployment option, and set up monitoring of our application.

In the next chapter, we're going to look at some real-world architectures. This chapter will act as a complement to the hands-on chapters and will hopefully give you some ideas for new real-time analytics applications to build.

CHAPTER 12

Real-Time Analytics in the Real World

This chapter presents some real-world reference architectures so that you have other examples of how to glue the various parts of the real-time analytics stack together, in addition to what we've covered in the worked example part of the book. These architectures will complement the one that we built in the hands-on section of the book.

We will be using fictional companies, but the architectures are based on ones that are being used in production.

Content Recommendation (Professional Social Network)

MySpot is a popular (but fictional!) social network that lets users find and interact with people in their professional network. It offers users a suite of tools that makes it easier for people to find others who have the same interests or who may be interested in collaborating on projects. See Figure 12-1.

MySpot's main interface is a news feed that shows a selection of content, including articles, job announcements, job postings, and other topics that might be of interest.

Users can engage with others' content by choosing to react, share, or comment. These interactions not only foster communication among professionals but also provide valuable input for MySpot's personalization algorithm. The more users engage with the platform, the better MySpot's algorithm can tailor their news feeds to suit their unique needs and preferences.

NAME
MySpot

INDUSTRY
Professional social network

PROBLEM
Content being shown on the news feed is stale and isn't being interacted with as much as the product team would like.

Figure 12-1. MySpot

On top of this, MySpot also offers other features you'd expect to see on a social network, like private messaging and group discussions, making it easy for users to build connections and collaborate on projects.

The Problem

MySpot wants the news-feed content to be relevant to its users. While more than enough content is being generated, working out what to show is still a challenge.

Users visit MySpot multiple times a day, and the customer success team has been receiving complaints that they are seeing the same, often stale, content multiple times. These complaints were corroborated by looking at the data, which showed that users were interacting with news-feed posts less often as time went on.

MySpot's management team feels that the natural conclusion of this trend will be that users will stop using the platform. This would have a domino effect on advertisers not wanting to place advertisements anymore, which would have a negative impact on revenue generation.

The Solution

MySpot has decided that it needs to address two main problems:

- Prevent users from seeing the same item that they've already seen or interacted with more than $<n>$ number of times.
- Don't show users items that are more than $<m>$ days old.

The data required to solve this problem can be collected when a user consumes items in the news feed. MySpot collects data on views, comments, and likes of an item.

Here is an example of one of these events:

```
{
  "userId": "a0e4a5d0-ad35-11ed-afa1-0242ac120002",
  "contentId": "b14dcd02-ad35-11ed-afa1-0242ac120002",
  "action": "VIEWED",
  "timestamp": "2023-02-12T13:37:11+00:00"
}
```

These events are streamed into a data streaming platform, using either an event tracker or a language SDK. An aggregation transformation is then applied to the events by a stream processor.

The aggregation transformation counts the number of interactions between a user and a piece of content within a given window. If a user views and shares a piece of content, this counts as two interactions. The events that eventually make their way to the serving layer look like this:

```
{
  "userId": "a0e4a5d0-ad35-11ed-afa1-0242ac120002",
  "contentId": "b14dcd02-ad35-11ed-afa1-0242ac120002",
  "interactions": 3
}
```

An application server than sends some queries to the serving layer to work out which items to render on the user's news feed. One of these queries will find out how many times a user has seen a provided list of items. Based on the result returned by that query, the application server can apply a dampening factor to those items to reduce the likelihood of them appearing high up in a user's feed.

Since this solution will be used in a feature that has high traffic, and MySpot's users are quite impatient, the solution must support both high throughput and low latency.

The architecture used by MySpot is shown in Figure 12-2.

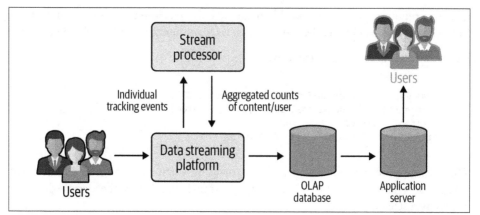

Figure 12-2. MySpot architecture diagram

Benefits

As a result of implementing this new architecture, MySpot's users are happier and are seeing more relevant content. News feed metrics are showing increased engagement, and the company is seeing users spend more time browsing the feed.

The customer support team is happy as well because users are no longer complaining about the news feed in their feedback.

Operational Analytics (Streaming Service)

StreamDream is a (made-up!) streaming service that provide access to a range of movies, TV shows, and original programming for tens of millions of subscribers. See Figure 12-3.

Figure 12-3. StreamDream

StreamDream offers this service via its website and an application that's available in both the Google Play and Apple stores. It is also available on a range of streaming devices, including smart TVs, Roku, Amazon Fire TV Stick, and Apple TV.

The application itself includes a recommendation engine so that it can make personalized content suggestions to users based on their viewing history and preferences.

The Problem

StreamDream is constantly pushing updates to its application and wants to make sure these updates are not harming the viewer experience. The company also wants to know whether the changes are having the desired impact.

The software updates are first pushed out to a set of canary users and then, if all the metrics look fine, they are pushed out to the rest of the users. At the moment, this process is a bit slow, and it takes too long to roll updates out to all users. In addition, bugs have been released and StreamDream hasn't found out until complaints are reported via the customer service team.

StreamDream would like to get to a position where it can get real-time operational metrics so that it can assess the impact of software updates. In an ideal world, the company would be able to roll out updates to all users after only a few hours of canary testing, with a high degree of confidence that there aren't going to be any problems.

The Solution

StreamDream is going to solve this problem by building a real-time analytics application on top of the log data that is already being collected from playback devices. This data is usually fed into a batch data pipeline and consumed by the analytics team the next day, but now it will form the backbone of a real-time analytics dashboard used by the operations team.

Here is an example of a log message collected from a device:

```
{
    "userId": "123456789",
    "deviceInfo": {
        "model": "Fire TV Stick 4K Max",
        "operatingSystem": "FireOS",
        "firmwareVersion": "7.6.1.4",
        "screenResolution": "1080p"
    },
    "appVersion": "2.5.2",
    "userActions": {
        "searchQuery": "Comedy movies",
        "selectedContentId": "530975",
        "playbackPosition": "00:12:02"
    },
    "playbackInfo": {
        "videoQuality": "HD",
        "bufferingTime": "7 seconds",
        "bitrate": "11 Mbps"
    },
    "errorMessage": {
        "errorCode": "500",
        "message": "Server Error"
    }
}
```

These events are sent from the device to the log API server, which is responsible for streaming them to the data streaming platform.

The initial data that was ingested has user details attached, but for this use case we don't need it, so the data was anonymized by the stream processor. The anonymized data is written to a new topic, which is ingested into an OLAP database, as shown in Figure 12-4.

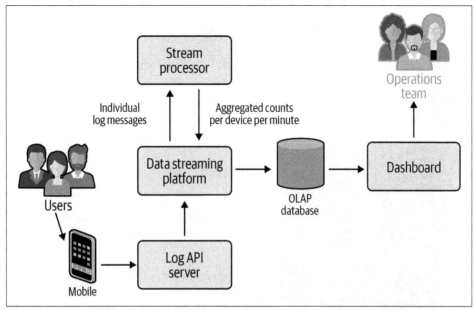

Figure 12-4. StreamDream architecture diagram

The operations team is served the data via a dashboard that queries the OLAP database. The dashboard shows any errors that have occurred during the rollout, as well as performance data grouped by device, firmware version, application version, and resolution. The operations team also receives alerts is a big drop occurs in any of the key metrics.

Benefits

As a result of introducing real-time analytics, StreamDream can now see exactly what's happening when it rolls out software updates. On a couple of occasions, the company has been able to quickly roll back a change after seeing dips in usage on certain devices that it hadn't been picked up on.

The engineering team is happy that they now have a way of seeing whether new features are having the desired impact. This will make it easier for them to evolve the application over time. The customer support team is also happy now that rolling out new releases doesn't automatically result in more work for them!

Real-Time Ad Analytics (Online Marketplace)

TreasuredGoods is a fictional online marketplace that connects buyers and sellers from around the world (see Figure 12-5). The platform offers a wide variety of hand-made, vintage, and rare products that can't be found elsewhere.

NAME
TreasuredGoods

INDUSTRY
Online marketplace connecting buyers and sellers of rare products

PROBLEM
Can't show up-to-date data on advert performance. Sellers are frustrated and might stop using the ad platform.

Figure 12-5. TreasuredGoods

The majority of the sellers are small businesses or individuals. Buyers can browse and purchase goods via a website or mobile phone app. Buyers can engage with sellers, ask questions, and leave reviews to help others make informed purchases.

In addition to taking a commission on every sale, TreasuredGoods generates revenue by placing advertisements throughout the app. These ads are placed by sellers, and the majority are on the category and individual product pages, as this is where the best targeting is possible.

The Problem

TreasuredGoods provides its sellers with a dashboard that shows how well their ads are performing. The sellers are able to see the number of impressions on an ad, the click-through rate, cost per click, on which pages their ads were placed, as well as a breakdown of who the ads are being shown to.

The ad platform initially had a slow take-up, so TreasuredGoods made the decision to store ad tracking data on a read-only replica of its operational database. The company already had considerable expertise with this database and was therefore able to get a first version of the dashboard up and running quickly.

As time has gone by, the volume of ads has increased, and it's become increasingly difficult to provide timely data on ad performance. Sellers would also like more flexibility over the way that they slice and dice the data, which isn't possible with the current architecture because the data has already been preaggregated for performance reasons. The sellers are frustrated, and some of them are wondering whether they should stop using the ad platform.

The Solution

TreasuredGoods is going to solve this problem by using real-time analytics.

The company is already capturing data about the advertisements shown to buyers into a streaming data platform. Here is an example of a message:

```
{
    "timestamp": "2023-03-14T16:54:00Z",
    "userId": "231491",
    "advertId": "76001",
    "advertFormat": "banner",
    "placement": "homepage",
    "timesViewedBefore": 3,
    "clickedThrough": "true"
}
```

In the current system, these messages are processed in a batch processing pipeline, and then windows are created over the data to capture 1-, 5-, and 10-minute rolling counts of the impressions, before the results are stored in a relational database.

In the new architecture, we're going to keep the full event payload, apart from user_id, for drill-down purposes. We'll convert user_id to user_bucket to give a view into the types of users who viewed the ads without revealing their identities.

This data transformation will be done by a stream processor. An example of a transformed message is shown here:

```
{
    "timestamp": "2023-03-14T16:54:00Z",
    "userBucket": "72",
    "advertId": "76001",
    "advertFormat": "banner",
    "placement": "homepage",
    "timesViewedBefore": 3,
    "clickedThrough": "true"
}
```

The resulting messages will be written to a new topic in the streaming data platform. That data will then be ingested into a real-time OLAP database, as seen in Figure 12-6.

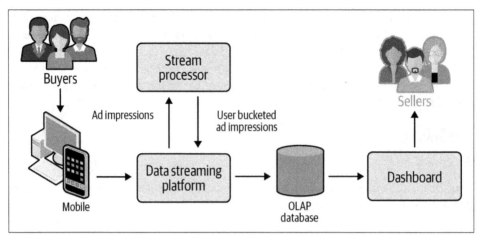

Figure 12-6. TreasuredGoods architecture diagram

The seller's dashboard then queries the data from the OLAP store.

Benefits

The sellers are the primary beneficiaries of the introduction of real-time analytics. The dashboard is now current within a few seconds, which makes it much easier for sellers to make decisions about where and when they want to place ads.

Since we are now storing a much finer-grained version of impressions data, the front-end team has been able to update the UI to give the sellers more control over the data that they're viewing. The customer support team is also happy, as sellers have stopped submitting tickets complaining about stale data!

User-Facing Analytics (Collaboration Platform)

VortexMeet is an imaginary and yet innovative collaboration platform specifically designed for tech companies, offering an extensive suite of tools that facilitate whiteboarding, pair programming, code reviews, and more (see Figure 12-7). The majority of VortexMeet's customers are operating in a remote or hybrid work setup, and the platform is therefore essential for ensuring that employees can collaborate with one another.

NAME
VortexMeet

INDUSTRY
Collaboration platform focused on tech companies

PROBLEM
Users aren't making VortexMeet an integral part of their workday, which makes them a flight risk.

Figure 12-7. VortexMeet

At the heart of VortexMeet is a revolutionary whiteboarding functionality that lets users draw, write, and share multimedia in real time by using an intuitive interface. What sets VortexMeet apart from its competitors is the low latency of the platform; it feels almost like you're working on a real-life whiteboard and not one in a web browser.

VortexMeet also has the basics that you'd expect in any collaboration platform, including high-quality video and audio conferencing, screen sharing, and chat. The combination of all these tools in one platform helps their customers improve better communication and productivity across the business.

The Problem

Users are generally happy with VortexMeet, as it works well for them and removes a lot of problems that they had with previous platforms. VortexMeet collects a lot of telemetry data and is therefore able to address any problems with performance before users are aware there's an issue.

Despite this, VortexMeet's product team is concerned that users aren't getting the full benefit from the platform. A considerable number of users use VortexMeet for only a couple of hours a day, which doesn't fit with VortexMeet's mission of becoming an integral part of its users' daily work routines and lives.

The Solution

To solve this problem, the product team would like to add some new data products that will give users insight into the way that they're using the platform and help them schedule collaboration sessions with colleagues.

We'll start by collecting events that describe the activities that users can do on the platform. Here are a couple of examples:

```
{
  "eventType": "meetingAttended",
  "timestamp": "2023-03-15T15:02:04Z",
  "userId": "711454d0-d989-4531-a603-c5b6dd5f96c3",
  "meetingId": "227ad5d0-5b46-4110-8eb4-46b44d5f601f",
  "meetingDuration": 60,
  "participants": [
    "db8bd7ac-7d68-4ee7-b0d4-62f5f00455ed",
    "a73291b0-462c-4a67-9db3-19fc8b0da081",
    "04aadaca-3c83-4436-8ee0-85ff1d5e3e85"
  ]
}

{
  "eventType": "pairProgrammingSessionEnd",
  "timestamp": "2023-03-15T15:13:01Z",
  "sessionId": "550e8400-e29b-41d4-a716-446655440001",
  "teamId": "c8d63140-0df2-46d5-bb87-8aa93e9c1e10",
  "usersInvolved": [
    "6ba7b810-9dad-11d1-80b4-00c04fd430c8",
    "04aadaca-3c83-4436-8ee0-85ff1d5e3e85"
  ],
  "sessionDuration": 45
}
```

These events will be ingested into the streaming data platform, as shown in Figure 12-8.

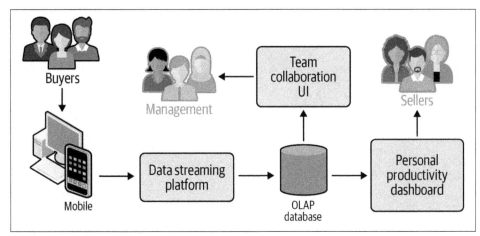

Figure 12-8. VortexMeet architecture diagram

The data will then be ingested into an OLAP database, from which the engineering team can build any number of user-facing applications. Although those applications won't be accessible on the internet, they will still have a lot of concurrent (and impatient!) users—VortexMeet's largest customers have tens of thousands of employees.

There is also the potential in the future to build internal-facing applications on this data that could be used by VortexMeet's account managers to keep track of their customers' usage and satisfaction levels.

Benefits

The product team's metrics are all looking good. They're seeing more usage per day, and most users are now using the platform almost every workday. They are also seeing more usage of the whiteboarding and pair programming platform after adding a tool to make it easier to schedule sessions.

The management team is happy as well and is confident that real-time analytics has helped extend VortexMeet's lead over the competition and will lead to more users in the future.

Summary

In this chapter, we've explored a series of real-world use cases disguised by imaginary company names. Hopefully, these examples acted as a useful complement to the hands-on pizza shop example that ran through the earlier part of the book.

In the next chapter, we'll look at the future of real-time analytics, including interesting technologies that I think will come to the fore in the next few years.

CHAPTER 13

The Future of Real-Time Analytics

So far in this book, we have discussed the current state of real-time analytics systems, and we've covered a lot of ground, learning about a lot of technologies. The adoption of real-time analytics is expected to grow exponentially over the next few years as more businesses become more data driven, and the technologies used to make real-time analytics become more accessible and easier to use.

While I don't have a crystal ball, in this chapter we'll look at where this field might go in the next few years. We'll also briefly describe technologies that will make real-time analytics more affordable and accessible to businesses and end users.

Edge Analytics

The IoT has already permeated many aspects of our daily lives, but it is expected to become even more ubiquitous in the coming years. With the proliferation of IoT devices, the amount of data generated is staggering, and managing and making sense of this data will be a critical challenge. This is where real-time analytics will play a crucial role.

Edge analytics is the process of analyzing data at or near the edge of the network, where the data is generated. This is in contrast to *traditional analytics*, which typically involves sending data to a centralized location for processing. Figure 13-1 shows a typical architecture for edge analytics.

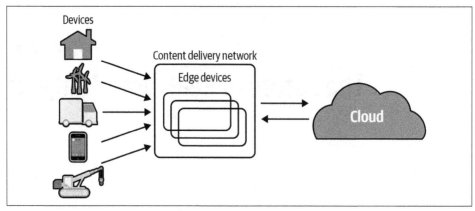

Figure 13-1. Edge analytics architecture

Edge analytics allows organizations to analyze data in real time, enabling faster decision making and reducing the amount of data that needs to be sent over the network. This approach is especially useful when low latency and real-time analysis are critical, such as in industrial IoT applications, where decisions must be made quickly based on sensor data.

One of the breakthrough technologies of the last year is DuckDB, an embeddable, columnar, analytical database system designed for fast analytical queries. It has packages for R, Python, and, intriguingly, Wasm. At the moment, it's focused on querying batch storage formats, but it would be interesting to see it implement the functionality to query streams of data in the future. I could see the Wasm package being embedded in applications deployed to the edge, performing fast analytical queries in the browser.

Regardless of the technology that gets used, by integrating real-time analytics with IoT, businesses will be able to gain even deeper insights into their operations and make more informed decisions.

Compute-Storage Separation

A primary challenge for real-time analytics systems is figuring out how to deal with an ever-growing dataset while keeping costs under control and meeting query SLAs. The separation of compute from storage has become a standard practice for solving this problem in real-time analytics systems, enabling organizations to achieve the following benefits:

Scalability

Separating compute and storage means that we can scale each independently. If our application needs more compute power but doesn't require additional storage space, we can buy more compute while leaving our storage as it is.

Flexibility

We can choose different types and sizes of compute resources depending on our workload, without affecting our data. This enables us to choose suitable compute resources for the tasks that need doing.

Cost-effectiveness

When storage and compute are coupled and we want to increase the amount of one, we also have to pay to increase the amount of the other, even if we don't use it. That problem goes away with separation.

Compute-storage separation also lets us allocate resources more efficiently. By decoupling storage from processing, we can independently scale compute resources to handle fluctuating workloads without affecting the storage layer. This results in better resource utilization and cost optimization, since resources can be provisioned and de-provisioned as and when required.

One problem created by separating storage and compute is that we add latency because we're moving data around. To make queries that use this architecture performant, it's crucial to implement predicate pushdown optimization. *Predicate pushdown* is where we push the WHERE clause down into the storage layer and do data filtering at that layer so that we send back only the minimum data required. As Gwen Shapira points out in her post "Compute-Storage Separation Explained" (*https://oreil.ly/4ikAD*), if we don't implement predicate pushdown, we may find that the network between the compute and storage nodes becomes a bottleneck. Predicate pushdown is therefore an important optimization that works in lockstep with the separation of compute and storage.

Tiered storage is a popular approach that helps analytics systems separate out compute and storage. It does this by offloading older data into a cheaper, more reliable storage medium like cloud object stores such as Amazon S3 and Google Cloud Storage, while keeping only the most recent data in local storage, which is faster but more expensive.

Many of the tools that form part of the real-time analytics stack, including Apache Kafka and Apache Pinot, have started supporting tiered storage features to reduce the total cost of ownership (TCO) while running in production. Figure 13-2 shows Pinot's tiered storage architecture.

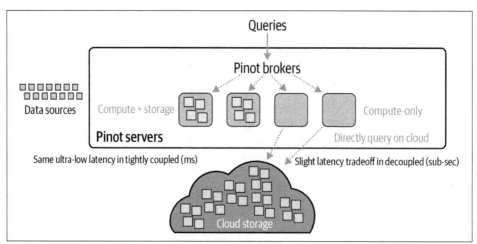

Figure 13-2. Apache Pinot's tiered storage

Tiered storage provides the best of both worlds in terms of cost and query performance, as shown in Figure 13-3.

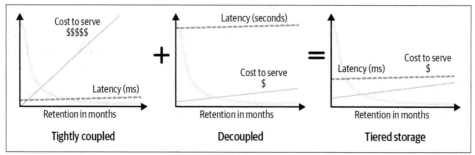

Figure 13-3. The best of both worlds

Queries won't be as fast as they would be if we tightly couple storage and compute, and the latency won't be as high as if we stored all data (both hot and cold) in cheaper storage. Instead, we get reasonably fast queries with much reduced storage costs.

Data Lakehouses

A *data lakehouse* is a modern data architecture that builds upon the best ideas of data lakes and data warehouses. It keeps the flexibility and openness of storage format that made data lakes popular, but on top of that it introduces transactions and schema evolution, which were limitations in data lakes.

A data lakehouse is designed to enable organizations to store and manage large volumes of structured and unstructured data in a centralized location, while also providing the ability to process and analyze it in real time. Data lakehouses provide a more flexible and scalable approach to data management than traditional data warehouses, while also providing a higher level of data governance and security than data lakes. They are becoming increasingly popular among organizations that need to analyze large volumes of data in real time to gain insights and make informed decisions.

Figure 13-4 shows the architecture of Delta Lake, a popular open source data lakehouse.

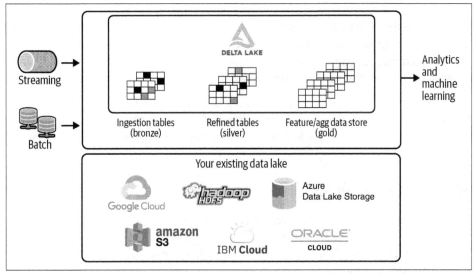

Figure 13-4. Delta Lake architecture

While data lakehouses are designed with data at rest in mind, they could be combined with real-time analytics to generate insights with more accuracy.

Data lakehouses can keep past data records for many years, including the complete audit history and the full view of the changes. Real-time analytics systems can leverage this richness of data lineage by federating queries to lakehouses via connectors.

At the time of writing, StarTree Cloud includes a Delta Lake connector for ingesting data into Apache Pinot. ClickHouse has functionality that lets users create a read-only integration with Delta Lake, Apache Hudi, and Apache Iceberg.

It will be interesting to see if other real-time OLAP stores follow their lead. I also wonder if we'll end up with tighter integration between lakehouses and the real-time analytics ecosystem as time goes on.

Real-Time Data Visualization

Data visualization is considered the last mile of real-time analytics. It helps human users better understand and react to the insights generated by real-time analytics systems.

Today, many business intelligence (BI) suites are already making exploratory data analysis a better experience for analysts and end users. Unfortunately, real-time visualization has a long way to go.

The support for interactivity, such as drill-downs and slicing and dicing real-time data, will be a great addition to real-time data visualization systems. Moreover, they can be made more scalable to enable the visualization of large volumes of data in real time without experiencing performance issues.

However, several BI vendors are increasing their offerings to add support for rich real-time data visualizations. Although most of them are in the operational analytics and monitoring space, they will become more popular in general data engineering spaces.

Streaming Databases

A *streaming database* that can process and analyze data in real time as it is generated, rather than storing it first and then processing it later. Streaming databases are not an entirely new concept— they combine the capabilities of a stateful stream processor and a database to bring the best of both worlds.

The stream processor capabilities enable *streaming data ingestion*—the ability to consume data from a stream and persist it continuously. The database capabilities enable fault-tolerant state persistence, data-indexing strategies, and efficient ad hoc querying on stored data. The architecture of a streaming database is shown in Figure 13-5.

Having a streaming database in your architecture unlocks several real-time analytics use cases and helps reduce the infrastructure footprint as well. For example, streaming databases eliminate the need for time-consuming batch ETL pipelines, which would ingest data first, clean it, and then load it into databases to run analytics later. The stream processing portion of streaming databases supports streaming ETL on the data arriving, allowing cleanup and transformations before persisting the data. That results in increased data freshness, with low latency between the time data is ingested and the time that insights are generated.

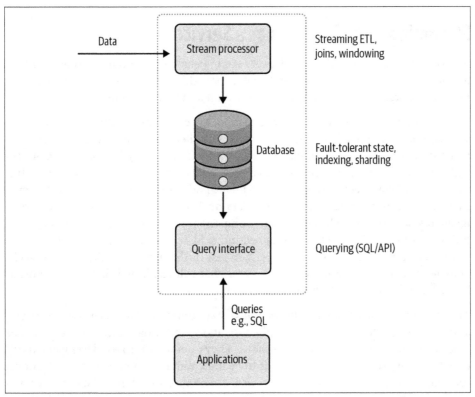

Figure 13-5. Streaming database architecture

Many streaming databases, specifically those released recently, have adopted a wire format (a communication protocol) compatible with most relational databases. For example, PostgreSQL wire format has been adopted by streaming databases vendors such as Materialize. This allows clients to query these tools as if they were querying a regular PostgreSQL database.

Streaming databases blur the lines between databases and stream processors and also lower the barrier for small organizations to benefit from real-time analytics in a simpler and more cost-efficient manner.

Streaming Data Platform as a Service

As I've stated, we can build a modern streaming stack by combining components of multiple vendors, technologies, and platforms. Although that's great flexibility for most, some organizations prefer everything built and managed under one roof.

A data platform may consist of various technology components. Building, managing, and owning such a platform will soon become challenging as the number of components starts to grow. For example, you can start with a minimal viable data platform with a cloud-hosted data warehouse, data lake, data orchestration tool, and a BI infrastructure. As your requirements grow, you will add more components to this mix, such as a streaming data platform or a data quality-control tool. The data platform inevitably becomes complicated as each component requires different levels of monitoring, hardware, licensing, and engineering skill set to manage in the long term. Moreover, technology adoption happens so fast in the data space that existing technologies can be outdated in just a few years. That will result in a skill-sourcing problem, especially for legacy technologies.

This is where *streaming data platform as a service* comes in. These platforms offer you a comprehensive tool belt to plan, build, test, and monitor data-intensive applications at scale without the management overhead. They offer an improved developer experience to declaratively define what needs to be done rather than how it should be done. As a developer, you can use standard SQL (or Python) to define data sources and sinks, the transformations applied to the data, and the queries that produce the required metrics you need. The rest will be taken care of by the platform, such as scaling up and down based on demand, security, monitoring, and upgrades, which would've taken a significant portion of your time and budget.

DeltaStream and Decodable are two companies trying to realize this concept, making real-time analytics accessible and affordable for the masses. Figure 13-6 shows Decodable's platform (*https://oreil.ly/FAWAD*).

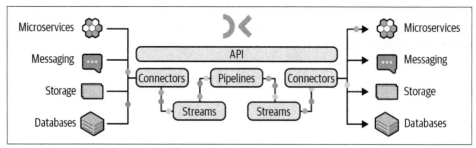

Figure 13-6. Decodable platform

As you can see, pipelines, streams, and connectors are all encapsulated inside the platform. Developers can configure everything by using Decodable's UI, and transformations are written in SQL. These types of platforms will help democratize the modern streaming stack.

Reverse ETL

As the name suggests, *reverse ETL* tools perform ETL backward (see Figure 13-7). They extract the generated insights from data warehouses, transform them, and sync them back to the operational systems (such as CRMs, marketing automation tools, and other applications) where the data originated. With these tools, companies can create a closed-loop data cycle that enables them to make more informed decisions and take action in real time based on the insights derived from their data.

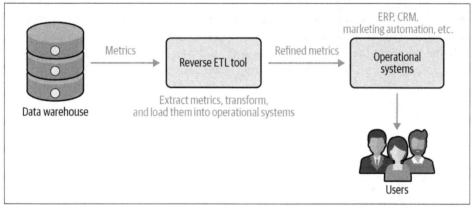

Figure 13-7. Reverse ETL architecture

Reverse ETL is particularly useful for companies that have invested heavily in building a centralized data infrastructure to support analytics and reporting but have struggled to turn those insights into action. By syncing data back to operational systems, companies can ensure that insights derived from their data are put into practice, resulting in improved customer experiences, more effective marketing campaigns, and better business outcomes overall.

To put reverse ETL into perspective, let's consider a real-world example: ecommerce companies. Ecommerce companies often have a wealth of customer data stored in their data warehouses, including information about customers' purchase histories, browsing behaviors, and demographic information.

Using a reverse ETL system, ecommerce companies can sync this data back to their operational systems, such as their marketing automation tools or CRM systems, to create more personalized and targeted marketing campaigns. For example, a company might use the data from its data warehouse to identify customers who have recently abandoned their shopping carts and then use a marketing automation tool to send targeted emails to those customers, offering them discounts or other incentives to complete their purchases.

A plethora of reverse ETL platforms are available, including Rivery, Hightouch, Census, Polytomic, and Integrate.io.

Summary

Real-time analytics applications have become increasingly vital in today's data-driven world, as they allow businesses to process, analyze, and act on data in real time. Whether monitoring customer behavior or predicting equipment failure, the use cases for real-time analytics applications are vast and ever-expanding.

The technology landscape of real-time analytics is diverse and dynamic—it tends to change faster than you imagine. With advancements in technology and the growing number of data sources, we will inevitably see frequent innovations in this space. Whether to adopt these trends or not is your decision, which you should make based on factors such as primary use cases, budget, and your team's current skill set.

Index

About the Author

Mark Needham is an Apache Pinot advocate and developer advocate at StarTree. Mark helps users learn how to use Apache Pinot to build their real-time, user-facing analytics applications. He also does developer experience, simplifying the getting-started experience by making product tweaks and improvements to the documentation. Mark writes about his experiences working with Pinot at *markhneedham.com*. He tweets as @markhneedham (*https://twitter.com/markhneedham*).

Colophon

The animal on the cover of *Building Real-Time Analytics Systems* is a common buzzard (*Buteo buteo*), also known as a Eurasian buzzard. It is a medium-sized raptor, with a wingspan between about three and a half and four and a half feet.

The common buzzard's resident range covers much of Europe and parts of the Middle East, with a breeding range stretching into central Asia. It is considered a partial migrant, with some populations generally wintering in warmer regions, though there is considerable variation even at the individual level. Populations in colder regions generally winter in central or southern Europe, though some migrate as far as southern Africa. Other populations move widely throughout the year as food resources change, while some remain largely in the same area year-round.

The common buzzard is classified as a species of least concern. It is one of the most numerous birds of prey in its range, and its numbers have increased in recent years thanks to conservation efforts. Many of the animals on O'Reilly covers are endangered; all of them are important to the world.

The cover illustration is by Karen Montgomery, based on an antique line engraving from *British Birds*. The cover fonts are Gilroy Semibold and Guardian Sans. The text font is Adobe Minion Pro; the heading font is Adobe Myriad Condensed; and the code font is Dalton Maag's Ubuntu Mono.

Printed in the USA
CPSIA information can be obtained
at www.ICGtesting.com
JSHW051438270923
49259JS00005B/31